The Leader's Tool Kit

The Leader's Tool Kit

Hundreds of Tips and Techniques for Developing the Skills You Need

Cy Charney

American Management Association

New York • Atlanta • Brussels • Chicago • Mexico City • San Francisco
Shanghai • Tokyo • Toronto • Washington, D.C.

Special discounts on bulk quantities of AMACOM books are available to corporations, professional associations, and other organizations. For details, contact Special Sales Department, AMACOM, a division of American Management Association, 1601 Broadway, New York, NY 10019.
Tel.: 212-903-8316. Fax: 212-903-8083.
Web site: www.amacombooks.org

This publication is designed to provide accurate and authoritative information in regard to the subject matter covered. It is sold with the understanding that the publisher is not engaged in rendering legal, accounting, or other professional service. If legal advice or other expert assistance is required, the services of a competent professional person should be sought.

Library of Congress Cataloging-in-Publication Data

Charney, Cyril.
    The leader's tool kit : hundreds of tips and techniques for developing the skills you need / Cy Charney.
      p. cm.
   Includes index.
   ISBN 0-8144-0847-8 (pbk.)
   1. Leadership.   I. Title.

HD57.7.C4756   2006
658.4'092—dc22

                                        2005011788

Printing number

10   9   8   7   6   5   4   3   2   1

Contents

Preface

Chances are you're probably not expecting to retire from your current place of employment. You're most likely going to look for greener pastures elsewhere. Or you may be put out to pasture against your will. If that day has come—or when it comes—how would you like to be remembered? Will people think of you as a leader or as a manager, a person who inspired and brought the best out in people or someone who plodded through each day fighting fires? Will you be remembered as someone who took your organization to new heights or someone who maintained the status quo? Will you be thought of as someone who held out a helping hand to those who needed it or someone who cared only about the bottom line?

This book is different from most that you'll find in your bookstore. Most leadership books focus on just a few aspects of leadership, claiming that visioning, inspiring, teamwork, or some other concept is *the* key to great leadership. And then they find some high-flying executive to deify as the embodiment of their theory. Baloney, I say! Leadership is complex. It requires people of great passion, vision, humility, generosity, and energy, people who spend their time in the service of others, finding and making heroes, creating long-term alliances, streamlining processes and operating ethically. And that is just the beginning. Leadership isn't something you learn in business schools. Analytical skills are useful, to be sure, but they don't give you the ability to influence people, to be passionate, or to adapt your style according to circumstances. These skills are learned from great mentors, in the school of hard knocks, and through trial and error. Hence this book will provide no easy formulas. Rather it will allow you, the reader, to pick and choose the tools and techniques you need for the situation you face, just in time.

Great leaders have many more attributes, some of which are situational and some of which are useful all the time. This book contains all the ingredients but gives you the ability to customize your learning by choosing the topics that are most applicable to you and to access the information as you need it. Clearly, this book is not the *War and Peace* of everything there is to know about leading. Rather, it is a collection of ideas collected over three decades of consulting and training, presented in the way that I most appreciate: quick hits that enable busy people either to gain new information or be reassured that they're on track.

To make this book the most useful one in your library, I have organized it by the types of activities that you as a leader should be focusing on: developing people, satisfying your stakeholders, operating your organization ethically, promoting continuous improvement, building a strong team of leaders, and communicating effectively. Some of these strategies will be easier for those readers at or near the top of their organization since these ideas are strategic and require considerable power and influence. But most of what you'll learn will be within the ability of managers at all levels to implement and will be especially useful for those on track to get to a senior level. Also, readers should see the linkage among many of the topics listed in the book and should review similar topics in order to get a rounded view of the challenges facing them.

This book is also written for people who realize that leaders are made, not born. The best leaders are often influenced by events that call on them to take up positions of power. What got them there and, more importantly, what sustained them at the top? In short, they had to craft their skills. They learned—from mistakes, from mentors, and from study. And they continued to learn, never believing for a moment that they had yet mastered the craft of leadership.

Acknowledgments

I would like to express my sincere thanks for the advice I received from a number of people and organizations. Larry Colero, president of Crossroads Programs Inc., in Vancouver, British Columbia, provided insight into strategic issues. John Platz, president of Platz & Associates Inc. and a renowned labor relations expert, offered me a unique perspective on union issues. Suzanne Sabourin, executive director of government relations at the Insurance Bureau of Canada, gave me insight into how to influence people in the public sector. Kathy Conway, president of Virtual Communications and my coauthor on *The Trainer's Tool Kit*, helped me better understand people-development strategies and the role of leaders in this process. Anna Armitage, manager of leadership development and learning at Siemens Canada, and Kathy Stein, director of human resource services for CallNet/Sprint Canada, both gave me invaluable advice on the issues of compensation and benefits—an area where I had little practical experience. Sheldon Silverman's combined background in law and technology were wonderful in appreciating the interaction of leadership and technology. Mark Gage of KPMG Consultants in Calgary, Alberta, shared his wisdom on the importance of strategies that make organizations more responsible to society and the environment. Finally, Peter Wright, director of transit operations for the City of Windsor, Ontario, provided particularly useful counsel on the topic of strategic direction.

I appreciate the guidance of my editor and friend, Adrienne Hickey, editorial director of AMACOM Books, whose high standards have forced me to labor longer on this book than any others I have written, ensuring that we have a book worthy of the AMACOM franchise.

Finally, I would like to acknowledge the work of my colleague Rosemary Kercz for her word-processing, editing, and research skills as well as Gillian Watts of Word Watch Editorial Services in Toronto.

The Leader's Tool Kit

PART 1

Leadership Fundamentals

Many acts of service cost nothing and take little time:
encouragement, compliments, listening, gratitude, and compassion.
Anytime you affirm the worth of others, you serve.

—Chris Karcher

Leaders are people of influence. Their enthusiasm and joy for what they do is infectious. It inspires others. Each day their work adds another layer to the foundations that build ever stronger organizations. They focus on developing competent, confident people who do the right thing daily. They focus on growing their organizations—not politics, career development, inflated stock values, or other distractions. They are rewarded by the journey. This section provides leaders with the tools to make this happen.

Adversity:
Coping with Tough Times

A journey of a thousand miles begins with a single step.

—Lao-Tzu

Everything I need to know, I learned from Noah's Ark:

1. Don't miss the boat.

2. Remember that we are all in the same boat.

3. Plan ahead. It wasn't raining when Noah built the Ark.

4. Stay fit. When you're 60 years old, someone may ask you to do something really big.

5. Don't listen to critics; just get on with the job that needs to be done.

6. Build your future on high ground.

7. For safety's sake, travel in pairs.

8. Speed isn't always an advantage. The snails were on board with the cheetahs.

9. When you're stressed, float awhile.

10. Remember, the Ark was built by amateurs; the *Titanic* by professionals.

11. No matter the storm, when you are with God, there's always a rainbow waiting.

—Author Unknown

Few organizations can continue to grow and expand without an occasional bump in the road. The difficulty may be short-lived or it may take a while to remedy. These setbacks will test your mettle as a leader because employees will be looking to you for reassurance that everything will be okay.

✓ Beware the grapevine! Employees will always see the worst in a situation when they suspect there is a problem but have little knowledge about what is happening. They will suspect a problem if:
- regular meetings are cancelled
- their managers disappear into meetings off-site or behind closed doors
- no one is saying anything about the current state of business, but overtime has been cancelled or a major contract has been lost

Without regular information from leadership, expect rumors to fly. And don't expect any of them to be good.

✓ Be honest and forthright in your communications. Hold information meetings with as many of the employees as possible so that everyone gets the same message at the same time. Be as honest as possible. At the same time, show the positive side of difficult decisions that have had to be made.

✓ Meet frequently with employees to solicit their ideas for change. The larger the employees' contribution to new procedures, the greater will be their buy-in and commitment.

✓ Ensure that you listen to employees and understand their concerns. Listening means more than simply hearing people's words. Listen to what they are feeling. Respond to the fears and anxieties that you detect in their body language as much as you pay attention to their verbal comments.

✓ Create an environment in which the criteria for success are known. Create certainty so that people know the goals, the limits of their decision making, and the guidelines by which they are expected to make those decisions. These steps will help remove uncertainties that eat away at superior performance.

✓ Demonstrate sacrifice. Be the first to volunteer for longer work hours or reduced pay.

✓ If layoffs are necessary, handle the process as humanely as possible.

Treat people with dignity so that they leave on as positive a note as possible.

✓ Deal with the aftermath of a layoff. Don't ignore the feelings—such as guilt—of the people left behind. Acknowledge those feelings and help people to move forward. Review with them the new business model that will produce more stability.

Authenticity

Every man builds his world in his own image. He has the power to choose,
but no power to escape the necessity of choice.

—Ayn Rand

Effective leaders are authentic. Authentic people don't try to pretend that they
are someone else. They are not phony. Their honesty, sincerity, and concern are
evident at all times. They aren't simply trying to imitate someone they hold up
as a role model. They don't have to pretend who they are.

- ✓ Authentic leaders are completely honest and participate in the here
  and now. Because they are genuine and sincere they earn the respect
  of the people around them.
- ✓ Authenticity involves many other qualities, such as being centered in
  yourself and with others, living comfortably with your own values and
  principles, and always feeling a sense of completeness in the meaning
  or purpose of your life.
- ✓ Inauthentic people lose touch with meaning; they don't have both feet
  on the ground. They can fall into chronic anxiety, boredom, and
  despair. To avoid the responsibility of living authentically they often
  seek quick fixes, such as anesthetizing themselves with alcohol or
  drugs to dull the pain of their reality. Some people assert that it's
  inauthentic to pursue any approach (from programs, books, etc.) that
  promises to help people transcend (escape?) the responsibilities—and
  sometimes the drudgery—of day-to-day living.

✓ The consequences of inauthentic behavior are significant, especially when it comes to trust. People are less likely to volunteer ideas or information the leader needs to know. They are more likely to question the leader's motives. They are less likely to give that leader 100-percent effort. These undercurrents sap the energy of people in the organization. The trust and camaraderie that provide emotional and spiritual fuel have a hard time blossoming.

✓ What causes leaders to be inauthentic? Here are some possibilities.

- *Personality Traits*. Some people come across as guarded or secretive because they are naturally cautious or reserved. When such a person is the formal leader, people tend to be uncomfortable because they're never quite sure what he is thinking or feeling. Individuals in leadership positions who have this kind of personality would do well to consider ways to reduce this uneasiness in others. Finding ways to communicate more openly and honestly, free of personal agendas, will go a long way toward improving trust and relationships. And communicating more often will make a difference too.

- *Expectations of Hierarchical, Bureaucratic, Organizational Models*. These models promote the belief that if managers show signs of being genuine and vulnerable, they are weak and ineffectual. Coupled with that is the belief that managers should have all the answers. But knowledge is not the source of power of really effective leaders. Ultimately, leadership is more about who you are than what you know.

✓ When inauthentic leaders try to create an image that they are not really capable of supporting, their people will see straight through it. Everybody is vulnerable. Nobody is perfect or invincible. Nor should we expect our leaders to be like Superman. The more self-confident a leader is, the easier it is to be vulnerable. Being self-confident also means that people can critique you without fearing that they will be attacked or expecting you to be defensive.

✓ Great leaders are passionate about their organizations and the futures of those organizations. Authenticity works hand in hand with passion—you can't project passion effectively without authenticity.

✓ Authentic leaders listen to their people. Successful industry leaders have demonstrated that if they are going to retain, inspire, mentor, and stretch today's workers, they have to hear what their people are saying. But hearing alone is not enough. A leader has to create opportunities and processes to ensure that discussions about the issues of the day can take place with an open spirit, both inside the organization and with outside stakeholders.

✓ Authentic leaders listen so that, if necessary, they can amend their understanding of a changing environment by being open to new information—no matter how frightening or personally distasteful it may be. This openness is demonstrated when leaders:
  • assess the capabilities of their organization's capacity
  • seek new strategies to meet new challenges and evolving circumstances
  • are able to abandon cherished ways of acting when new responses are required
  • amend their vision based on changing reality

✓ Authentic leaders are able to build trust. Trust is the cultural glue that holds networks of teams together. By demonstrating faith in others, the leader sets the example for his people to work together openly.

✓ Authentic leaders relish opportunities to learn through feedback. Listening to what is being said in the trenches provides a chance for a leader to move beyond her own expectations of what should be occurring, into what is *really* happening.

Change

Wisdom is knowing what to do next; virtue is doing it.
—David Starr Jordan

Change is the norm. Stability is out. Any organization that is not changing continuously will disappear, or it will have to undergo massive and painful reorganization to modernize its management practices. Ongoing change leads to innovation and adaptation. Not changing produces failure and periodic trauma, including outsourcing of jobs, closures, and downsizing. How can you, as a leader, promote ongoing change? Consider these actions:

✓ Create a vision and share it often with employees. Demonstrate your commitment by continuously behaving in a way that will move the organization closer to its ideal.

✓ Promote new initiatives that improve the organization.

✓ Involve people in discussions to improve commitment to change.

✓ Communicate reasons for decisions made when those decisions do not involve frontline employees.

✓ When desirable changes seem to be slowing or sputtering out, find out why. Identify roadblocks that have unexpectedly occurred, and remove them.

✓ Celebrate initiatives that aim to improve performance, whether they succeed or not.

✓ Include change and innovation as core competencies. Ensure that you have change agents, and that they are promoted into positions of influence.

✓ Provide training for all employees in skills that promote change. These skills include:
  - planning
  - goal setting
  - persuasion
  - problem solving
  - decision making
  - conflict resolution

✓ Establish measures of performance for both teams and individuals. Whatever gets measured will surely improve. Ensure that these indicators are also of importance to the stakeholders—customers, management, and employees.

✓ Get stakeholders involved in setting goals for all key indicators. Post the measures and goals where everyone can see them. Invisible measures and goals are unlikely to be met as well as those that are obvious to all.

✓ Celebrate measurable improvements at periodic (perhaps monthly) team meetings. Drop in on teams that have made significant improvements so that you can congratulate them.

✓ Send congratulations to departments, teams, and individuals that have contributed to successful new initiatives.

✓ Create annual awards for the most significant innovations.

✓ Set up systems to compare and share best practices among different parts of the organization.

✓ Communicate openly and frequently. Avoid secrecy unless it is absolutely essential. Post minutes of meetings on bulletin boards and your intranet. Hold communication meetings and encourage the inclusion of important information in the company newsletter.

✓ Recognize that not everyone can change equally quickly. Allow for adjustment time. Be empathetic with those taking a little longer to adjust to new circumstances.

✓ Provide training so that people can master new skills with confidence.

✓ Keep an eye out for people who are acting as roadblocks for change. Find out why they are behaving that way. Are their concerns legitimate? If so, respond to them. If not, and if their behavior has become an ongoing pattern, consider offering them opportunities for other work—elsewhere!

✓ Periodically (perhaps annually) evaluate your readiness for change. Among the most important contributors to change are:

- *Open Communication.* Is information readily available to people who need or want it?

- *Style of Management.* Is the company open and participative? Do you listen to your people? Do you take the time to achieve a consensus when time allows and commitment is needed?

- *Relationship with Union.* If you have a bargaining unit, do you work collaboratively with it? Have you avoided strikes or lockouts in the past? Does the company regard the union as a partner and key stakeholder or does it see it and treat union leaders as a necessary evil?

- *State of Business.* An organization that is growing at a steady pace is more likely to be able to embrace change than one that is faltering. It will usually have the funds and the enthusiasm to embrace change. Organizations that are in decline, even though they need and have the incentive to change, typically respond only to ruthlessly imposed change.

- *Atmosphere.* An informal culture that celebrates change and accepts mistakes as an opportunity to learn will constantly adopt new initiatives.

Collaboration and Teamwork

A mediocre idea that generates enthusiasm will go further than a great idea that inspires no one.

—Mary Kay Ash

Nothing influences behavior more than your behavior at the top. You are the role model and your actions, not the slogans on the wall, will influence how others behave. A collaborative environment that encourages working together for a common purpose, within and among teams, is important to your organization's success. Here are some strategies that will make this happen:

✓ Cultivate a cohesive team.
- When you have a choice, hire people with a positive, mature attitude toward their work and their colleagues. You will minimize the petty bickering, gossiping, and turf wars that distract good workers from concentrating their best energies on solving problems and getting the job done.
- Know when to step in and when to stay out of team conflicts. A certain amount of disagreement is normal in any team. But if a conflict between two or more employees is polarizing the group, interfering with communication (for example, employees refusing to speak to or work with each other), or using up an unacceptable amount of time and energy, it may be time for you to step in. If you don't feel you have the skills to mediate effectively between employ-

ees (or if you feel that you shouldn't be involved), consider bringing in a skilled mediator.

- Plan occasional team events that let people get together without the pressures of work. These might be a monthly lunch to celebrate team members' birthdays or a semiannual off-site planning day that includes time to socialize. Be creative if you have budget constraints. Ensure that these are events that everyone can participate in.

✓ Minimize the impact of a destructive team member. If you inherit a problematic employee or hire someone who turns out to have negative effects on the team's morale, find out what is interfering with that person's ability to be a positive, productive worker.

- If the problem is solvable (for example, maybe the person would be happier transferring to another area), do what you can to resolve the situation.
- If the person must stay, make clear your expectations for improvement and, if necessary, what the consequences might be if no improvement is forthcoming.
- If you are simply stuck with a negative employee whom you can't terminate, do what you can to minimize this person's effect on others (for example, assign tasks the employee can do on his own).

✓ Be loyal to your employees. Remember that loyalty is a two-way street.

- Be the voice of your team at the management table. If you don't promote their needs and give voice to their opinions, no one else will. However, ensure that your employees know it is your role to balance their needs with the needs of the organization.
- Share the credit with your team for its achievements and ensure that those above you know about its successes.
- Don't publicly point a finger when something goes wrong. If one or more team members have let the team down, address the situation with those people, but don't broadcast it at meetings or chastise the whole team for the actions of one or two.

✓ Promote team problem solving.
  - Strike a balance between sharing with your employees challenges that they need to know about and burdening them with or dwelling on problems they can't do much about.
  - Be accessible for consultation with your employees if problems arise, but don't micromanage. Encourage them to consult with each other for collaborative problem solving.
  - Establish a guideline that whenever employees bring you a problem, they are expected to also bring you at least one possible solution.

✓ Balance peak work periods with some rewards.
  - Recognize when your people are putting in extra effort. Acknowledge and thank them in a way that seems appropriate. Many people appreciate handwritten notes from the boss.
  - Give tangible rewards when it's practical and appropriate.
  - Celebrate the completion of a demanding project. Acknowledge special efforts or contributions made by individuals, but ensure that the team is also recognized as a unit.

✓ Help your employees to manage and learn from their challenges.
  - Find out what gets in the way of their doing their best. If red tape, bureaucracy, or politics interfere with their productivity, do what you can to buffer or eliminate those barriers.
  - Delegate, but don't abdicate. Giving your employees challenging problems to solve will help them to learn and grow, but ensure that they have (or can obtain) the knowledge, skills, and resources they need to handle these situations.

✓ Hold yourself to the same standards that you expect of others. Few people are inspired by someone who adheres to a double standard.
  - Don't ask your people to do anything you wouldn't do yourself.
  - Don't ask them to do anything illegal or unethical.

- Set standards that require people to stretch but aren't impossible to achieve.
- Give feedback in a fair, transparent manner. When you have concerns about an employee's performance, communicate and deal with those concerns directly with that team member. Don't express negative comments about a team member to other people on the team.

✓ Care about your people. You don't need to (nor should you) be their best friend or their personal counselor. However, getting to know them beyond saying "good morning" will allow you to find out what motivates and inspires them to give their all.
- Make small talk with your employees when the opportunity presents itself. Get to know more about their interests and goals and a bit of their personal lives, if they are willing to share.
- Greet employees by name when you make first contact each day. If you have a large number of employees, don't be afraid to ask them to remind you of their names if you forget. It shows you really want to remember them.
- Be a positive, encouraging force. When an individual or the team collectively seems tired or discouraged, express acknowledgment and appreciation for their efforts. Small gestures like a note of appreciation or even showing up with coffee and doughnuts at just the right moment can boost morale.

✓ Be willing to roll up your sleeves and work as hard as you expect your employees to work. In many cases your role is more appropriately that of a coach on the sidelines, but there may also be occasions when you have to get in the game yourself. Don't be afraid to get your hands dirty. You don't have to be down in the trenches every minute, but situations that call for extra manpower or superhuman effort are opportunities for you to inspire your people by working alongside them. The time when you stay until midnight along with the rest of the employees to finish a project or solve a problem is the stuff of corporate legends.

5

Communicating for Clarity and Commitment

Our lives begin to end the day we become silent about things that matter.
—Martin Luther King

No matter how many technological innovations for communication are invented, human beings will continue to have conversations to impart information. Given how long humans have been conversing, it is surprising that many people still have difficulty communicating verbally in their work environment. This is especially true when the conversation is between a manager and an employee. An effective leader will learn how to keep the conversation ongoing and the lines of communication open.

✓ Be accessible. Have an open-door policy.
  • Create an environment that encourages your people to speak to you.
  • Keep your office door open. Encourage your people to approach you at any time without the need to make an appointment. (Bear in mind that there will be times when you can't be interrupted. Make sure your employees know about and respect these occasions.)
  • Stroll around and speak with people casually.
  • Make an effort to learn something about each of your employees (for example, children's names, favorite pets, vacation destinations) and ask about these things, following up on previous conversations whenever possible.

✓ Pick the right moment to share ideas and listen to others.
  • Don't have conversations in a noisy area.
  • Find a time when no one is rushed or has an imminent deadline.
  • Don't do work or answer phone calls during conversations.
  • Turn all pagers and cell phones off or change them to "vibrate."

✓ Be aware of your part in the conversation.
  • Be specific and clear about what you want to discuss.
  • Choose your words carefully: Use "and" instead of "but" as a connector between sentences, and "I" or "we" statements instead of accusatory "you" statements.
  • Use bias-free language.
  • Vary your tone and delivery to emphasize certain points and to keep people interested. For important points, lean forward, open your eyes wider, and enunciate clearly.
  • Start the conversation off on a positive note, especially if the issue at hand is controversial.
  • Be brief but interesting.
  • Use humor or an anecdote to draw people in.

✓ Listen carefully to what people are telling you.
  • Don't interrupt, finish other people's sentences, or go on the defensive before someone has finished speaking.
  • Treat other people in the conversation with respect and encourage them to participate.
  • Be empathetic: If you can't agree with the substance of what someone is saying, try to understand and agree with her motivation for saying it.
  • Listen with your eyes.

✓ Wrap up the conversation with clarity.
  • Get confirmation on specific commitments ("It will be done on Fri-

day at three p.m." rather than "We'll get it done sometime before the end of the week").

- Paraphrase and summarize the main points of the conversation to make sure everyone else understands what has been said.

✓ Be mindful of how you dress.

- Your appearance communicates a message. If you want to impress the board members, dress like them. If you want to communicate with frontline people, dress more casually. This is particularly important for women. To appear professional, they should avoid clothing that is too tight, too short, too skimpy, or too low-cut for the standards of their business environment.

✓ Be assertive in your speech and actions.

- Don't ask for permission to pursue a new initiative unless it's a very big deal or the matter is out of your sphere of influence. Otherwise, simply let key people know what you're going to do. Show confidence and assume that all is okay unless you're advised to the contrary.

✓ Get to your point quickly.

- Long preambles are boring and wasteful. Verbal diarrhea makes people who should be paying attention let their minds wander.

✓ Market yourself constantly.

- Consider yourself as a brand. Stick to the brand you have created, whether it be as an innovator, strategic thinker, doer, or motivator. Constantly remind people—without being brash—what you bring to the table.

✓ Be proactive.

- Don't wait to be given what you need or want—ask for it before others do. This will show that you are thinking ahead.

✓ Be confident in your communication.

- Take calculated risks by making decisions before polling others to see what they think. Be an opinion maker, not a follower.

✓ Always be courteous and polite.

- But don't let others waste your time with gossip and useless chatter. Let them know that you have another commitment and have to leave.

Communicating One-on-One

Wisdom is the reward you get for a lifetime of listening
when you'd have preferred to talk.

—Doug Larson

The greatest mistake that leaders can make is to assume that, because of all their power, their employees believe them, agree with them, or have understood them. Communication problems happen all the time. But, with a little care and attention, many of these breakdowns can be avoided. We typically speak at between 100 and 200 words per minute, yet we are able to listen at many times that rate. But we find it difficult to have a meaningful conversation when the phone is ringing, e-mails are coming through, and others are trying to get our attention—all at the same time. Our ability to focus becomes compromised and it takes an enormous amount of energy and effort to listen to and receive a message clearly.

✓ The purposes of communicating are to gather information, give direction, show empathy, solve problems, make decisions, give encouragement, and share ideas.

✓ There are many barriers to effective communication. These barriers act as filters that prevent the message from getting through to the receiver, leading to delays, errors, and frustration. Being aware of them is the first step to overcoming them. These barriers include:

- *Noise.* Many workplaces are noisy because of machines, conversations, and outside traffic. We often have to wear earplugs to reduce the levels of noise. This makes it incredibly challenging to hold a conversation without shouting. Often the solution is to find a quiet spot or a quieter time, especially if the conversation is going to be protracted. If those options are unavailable, you will simply have to shout, but make sure you constantly summarize what you are hearing back to your conversation partner in order to avoid miscommunication.

- *Cultural Differences.* Workplaces are more multicultural than ever, especially in major metropolitan areas. It is not uncommon to find people from a dozen or more different backgrounds in a single organization. This presents an enormous challenge to anyone wanting to communicate effectively with everyone, as personal style invariably creeps into the process. It is necessary to maintain an objective, bias-neutral approach to each person, while making allowances for that person's culture. (See Chapter 38, "International Operations" for further ideas.)

- *Perceptions.* Our understanding and interpretation of messages are clouded by the "fog" that exists in our heads. This filtering of information is influenced by the level of stress we are under, as well as the values, knowledge, and experience that we bring to the information being communicated.

- *Typecasting.* Often we develop a schema, or mental pattern, that can taint our ability to communicate effectively. For example, if we typecast tech employees as laid-back, human resources people as "soft," design employees as flaky, or accountants as repressed bean counters, we are tempted to avoid challenging them with tasks outside their traditional spheres of interest or to ask for opinions on issues not related directly to their areas of expertise. However, many of the best ideas come from people who can see challenges from an outside, neutral perspective.

✓ The most important way to overcome obstacles to effective communication is to listen actively. Listening is far more difficult than it appears. People who listen with purpose typically:
  • spend less time talking
  • listen to be influenced rather than to rebut ideas
  • rarely start their sentences with "but"
  • understand any biases that they have and work consciously to overcome them
  • ask more open-ended questions
  • make notes to ensure that they have all the details
  • paraphrase often to confirm understanding and show that they have captured the essence of what has been communicated
  • do not finish other people's sentences

✓ Provide feedback. There is no point in having the other person guess how you feel about his idea. Let him know. But do so professionally, especially if you are not enamored of the idea. Focus on the issue, explaining specifically what you are not in favor of. Never make it personal. Demonstrate that you care about the other's input but that you have a problem with the idea. Ask for other ideas or different ways of modifying the idea to meet your criteria.

✓ One of the most effective ways to demonstrate listening is to pay attention to the meaning of the communication rather than to what is being said. The meaning is more often conveyed through nonverbal means, nuances, and body language. In fact, most communication is nonverbal, so to ignore this aspect is to miss most of what is being transmitted. Pay attention to a person's:
  • *Eyes*. It is said that the eyes are the windows to the soul. Losing eye contact or staring blankly may indicate a lack of interest in the conversation.
  • *Facial Expression*. A receptive receiver will smile and have a sparkle in his eyes. Your smile will indicate caring, empathy, and enthusiasm.

- *Voice Modulation*. A person may speak softly because of her cultural background, but a quiet voice can also indicate indecisiveness or uncertainty.
- *Proximity and Posture*. The way other people position themselves relative to you will indicate their interest in what you have to say. Standing closer rather than farther away, facing you, and leaning slightly forward will all demonstrate their interest in the discussion. However, cultural background may affect personal distancing during a conversation.

Communicating with Groups

So much of what we call management consists of making
it difficult for people to work.
—Peter Drucker

Any survey of unfulfilled needs in an organization will reveal inadequate communications. Communicating with employees is like filling a bottomless pit—there can never be enough.

How will followers judge their leaders? Foremost will be the amount and quality of communications.

✓ Many opportunities to communicate will present themselves, including:
  • informal interactions, such as conversations while walking around
  • formal interaction at small meetings
  • presentations at employees' information sessions, such as quarterly updates
  • presentations to stakeholders, such as suppliers, shareholders, or the board, aimed at winning support for change or a new project

✓ Time is money. Taking people away from their work for group meetings and information sessions is expensive. Leaders need to focus their communications on key issues that affect the performance of the organization and deal with issues of importance to their people. Typically these are:

- explaining the direction of the organization
- sharing strategies that will be used to achieve success
- letting people know the role they can play in achieving the goals
- updating employees on how the organization is doing and, more specifically, how their areas are performing
- providing recognition when appropriate

✓ Before holding a communications meeting with employees, ask yourself the following questions:

- *How often* should we hold these meetings? Monthly would be nice, but is it practical? Does our environment change so quickly that we need to bring everyone up to speed so frequently? Are there other ways of communicating important information in a way that everyone will understand?

- *What* information should I be sharing? How detailed should it be? How confidential is that information? More is better, for sure, and sharing confidential information does send a message that people can be trusted and are partners in the business.

- *Whom* should be invited? Should all the employees meet together or should they be separated so that they get different levels of information customized for their area's needs? For example, salespeople might need different information than operations employees.

- *Who* should present in a company-wide meeting? All senior managers should be involved in presenting their parts of the big picture from a variety of perspectives. However, if some of them have a problem being succinct and will take away from the time of others, it may be best to have one person do the entire "show."

- *Why* have the meetings? This is a no-brainer. Your employees deserve and need to know what's going on, how you're doing, what the future holds for them, and how anticipated changes might have an impact on their work lives.

- *Where* should we hold the meeting? Meeting rooms are often too small to hold a general town-hall type meeting. The cafeteria is one alternative, as it is usually big enough to hold most of the employees, although the ambiance is not particularly conducive to a serious meeting. Be sure to use the room that will have the fewest distractions and the lowest level of interfering noise.

✓ At the meeting ensure that you get the biggest bang for your buck by:
  • Keeping the presentation as short as is practical. Remember, most adults have a seven-minute attention span. So if the meeting goes beyond seven minutes, be sure to change the pace and keep it interactive. Moving on to new topics in quick succession will also maintain their attention.
  • Providing highlights without getting into too much depth, unless questions require it.
  • Making sure you are talking at the level of your audience.
  • Presenting the information in a way that indicates your understanding of the needs of the audience.
  • Walking around the room to ensure that you make eye contact with as many people as possible.
  • Encouraging questions, especially if you know that the issue being covered is a sensitive one.
  • Speaking slowly and clearly, especially if the audience is multilingual.
  • Complementing your presentation with PowerPoint slides, using graphs and pictures that strengthen the written words.
  • Using the words "we" and "us," suggesting that everyone is in the same boat. Using "me" and "you" suggests that you value the hierarchy and that you are different—perhaps better—than your audience.

✓ If you are dealing with a subject that might evoke some resistance, be prepared. Reduce the potential push-back by:
  • Balancing your presentation with a mixture of fact and emotions. Too much of either could sour the message. A good message tugs at the heart of your audience while providing factual information.

- Involving the audience. Try to engage their five senses so that they feel actively involved. This will create a more relaxed and receptive atmosphere.
- "Stroking" the audience. Let them know that you appreciate their support, loyalty, and efforts. This will create the expectation that past commitment will continue.
- Focusing on benefits before strategies. Let people know how they will be affected and the rewards for getting on board. The details can be shared later, when people are receptive to the change.
- Knowing who your opinion leaders are and doing whatever you can to get them on board before you share your message. Then they will not be surprised by the message and are less likely to criticize it publicly.
- Showing examples of where your plan has worked before. This will increase confidence that it has a chance of working this time.
- Running your ideas by some of the toughest critics in advance. Listen intensely to their criticisms and ensure that you are able to deal with them.
- Invoking the past, with examples of having overcome adversity and benefiting as a consequence.

✓ If people ask questions, handle them with care. Demonstrate your interest by:
- Repeating the question in your own words to ensure understanding and to let all know the issue in case they didn't hear the question.
- Showing no annoyance if the question is challenging. Demonstrate your class by focusing on the issue and not the person. Do not roll your eyes or show frustration; deal with the issue. At the end of your explanation confirm that the question has been answered satisfactorily and your answer understood.

Decision Making

A weak man always has doubts before a decision.
A strong man has them afterwards.

—Karl Kraus

How should decisions be made in fast-moving organizations? Should they be made by the people who are most qualified? Sure, but the matter is far more complex than that. Issues of governance abound. And in today's management culture we are expected to be more consultative. As a consequence, the following principles should be uppermost in your mind when decisions are being made.

✓ Consider who will be affected. Each stakeholder has different needs. Shareholders and the board want timely information and no unpleasant surprises. They expect to have little to do with day-to-day decisions, but they do need to be informed, if not invited, to give their opinions on major operational decisions. They always need to be involved in *strategic* decisions such as:
  - acquisitions
  - disposal of major assets
  - changes in executive management

✓ How about your union? Labor organizations feel strongly about being left out of important decisions that affect their members. They certainly need to be consulted about decisions that have an impact on the collective agreement. And if they are not involved in decisions outside of the collective agreement that affect their members, they should at least be informed about them as quickly as possible.

✓ And then there are the employees. People increasingly expect to be involved in decisions that affect them. And that makes good sense, as the results of decisions that involve employees are more likely to be implemented, and much faster too. So when should employees not be involved? Clearly, when:
- a decision needs to be made quickly
- health and safety are being compromised
- an expert opinion is required and available, rendering consultation and consensus superfluous

✓ The number of people who are affected by decisions will also influence how decisions are made.
- If the numbers are small, then a consensus is ideal especially if the group will need to implement the idea. A consensus is best achieved by:
  - presenting all the options to the group
  - allowing them to evaluate the pros and cons of each
  - narrowing down to the best choice
  - confirming that everyone can "live with" the idea
- For larger groups a majority vote is usually the best option. A vote gives everyone a say and can be done quickly.
- Minority decisions are always appropriate when:
  - one or a few people have specialized expertise
  - time is short
  - the decision is strategic
  - they have been assigned that task from the top
  - the decision has health, safety, or environmental implications that would land management in hot soup if there were a breach in regulations

9

Democratizing the Workplace

If liberty and equality, as is thought by some, are chiefly to be found in democracy, they will be best attained when all persons alike share in the government to the utmost.

—Aristotle

Leaders who create structures that enable people at all levels to participate in decisions benefit from improved morale, reduced turnover, higher productivity, and better customer service. This is not to say that employees should have an opportunity to participate in decision making all the time. Such opportunities occur when the issue has direct bearing on employees, there is time to get everyone's opinion, and the people participating are qualified in terms of knowledge and experience.

Here are some effective ways to unleash the power of an organization's people:

✓ For democracy to exist in the workplace, a special culture needs to be in place, one that:
  • stresses that participation is a part of the corporate culture rather than a program motivated by the training department
  • believes in the value of people and the contributions they can make

✓ Set up systems that enable the exchange of ideas. Problems should never be swept under the carpet. People should be encouraged to bring issues forward, together with ideas on how to correct them.

✓ Encourage all your managers to have regular meetings. These should ensure that:
  - information is shared openly
  - ideas are listened to, especially those that contribute to improvements in processes
  - employees are consulted about decisions, giving them some influence over when they will be affected

✓ Train all managers in skills that will ensure that they are participative. Ensure that they practice their learning by consulting employees about changes, informally as well as formally.

✓ Ensure that your training programs are always conducted within the framework of the organization's values of openness.

✓ Have suggestion boxes available so that people can offer ideas anonymously, should they choose to. Similarly, have dialogue venues on your intranet where people can post and discuss new ideas.

✓ Leave flip charts in various parts of the organization to encourage people to write down new ideas that can be investigated or discussed at departmental meetings.

✓ Hold town hall meetings where all the employees can gather for updates on how the organization is doing as well as changes that may be coming down the pike.

✓ Hire for attitude and train for skills. Choose managers who are willing to support an open work environment.

10

Ethics

Radical changes in world politics leave America with a heightened responsibility
to be, for the world, an example of a genuinely free, democratic, just and
humane society.

—Pope John Paul II

People look to you, as a leader, to model the behavior you expect of others. High
on the list is ethical behavior. Getting your head around ethics is like understanding good parenting—you know that it's desirable and worth the effort, but it's
hard to define specifically.

The temptation to cut corners and operate profitably in the short term,
at the expense of acting ethically in the long term, is always great. The tendency
to offer more benefits and favors to those closest to us (cronyism) is also powerful.
Here are some guidelines for ethical behavior:

✓ Understand that there are different types of ethical behavior.

Personal Ethics
These are the principles we try to instill in children. They include:
- concern about others
- respect for the autonomy of others
- honesty
- trustworthiness
- fairness
- benevolence

- prevention of harm
- sharing

Professional Ethics

Many professions have formal codes of conduct that, if broken, could lead to censure or even expulsion. They include concerns such as:
- impartiality
- openness and full disclosure
- confidentiality
- due diligence
- avoidance of conflict of interest
- fiduciary duty to protect and increase shareholder value

Global Ethics

Ethical principles are especially challenging for corporations that operate across borders. They include:
- respect for international and local laws
- social responsibility
- a holistic approach
- environmental stewardship

✓ Make ethical behavior a priority. Promote it in as many ways as possible, such as these:
- Define and document your company's ethical principles. Involve all the stakeholders in this process. Share these principles with everyone, ensuring that they are available and easily accessible. They should, for example, be part of orientation for new employees, in the employee handbook, on your Web page, and posted in offices and meeting rooms.
- Set up an ethics committee under a respected ombudsperson from outside the corporation to deal with grievances and conflicts.
- Do regular (annual) audits of corporate behaviors and compare the results to the documented ideal. Analyze the results, looking for gaps, and develop plans for improvement. Ensure that the process is open.

- Train and orient all employees on how to implement your codes of ethics and behavior.
- Include ethical behavior in performance reviews.
- Define consequences for those who do not operate according to the established principles.
- Empower and encourage employees to "blow the whistle" any time that behaviors, products, or services clearly contravene corporate standards.
- When judging new recruits on their competencies, include ethical behavior.
- Include ethical behavior as a criterion in decisions regarding promotions.
- Conduct regular verifications to ensure that claims made for products and services are accurate and true.
- Encourage the board of directors to approve systems that ensure compliance with the code of ethics.
- Involve the board of directors in periodic reviews and fine-tuning of the code of ethics.

✓ Build ethical standards into your dealings with the outside world, especially the customers.
  - Always promise realistic results. When providing a service be reasonable about expectations and suggest, as is often the case, that the best results tend to come from long-term, sustained efforts.
  - Don't look to make a quick killing in a situation where the buyer is somewhat naive. Sooner or later the truth will be told, and it may result in adverse publicity or expensive lawsuits. In any case, customers should be thought of as providing a steady stream of business over the long term.

Meetings

I love meetings with suits. I live for meetings with suits. I love them
because I know they had a really boring week and I walk in there with my
orange velvet leggings and drop popcorn in my cleavage and then fish it out
and eat it. I like that. I know I'm entertaining them and I know that they
know. Obviously, the best meetings are with suits that are intelligent,
because then things are operating on a whole other level.

—Madonna

Leaders spend a good portion of their time in meetings, and much of that time
is wasted. It is possible to cut meeting times in half, especially if you use a few
simple techniques. These techniques are important since as a leader you will set
the standard for meetings that others need to emulate.

1. Let people know in advance what the meeting is about. Send out an
   agenda showing:
   ✓ time and place
   ✓ meeting objectives
   ✓ items that will be dealt with
   ✓ any preparation needed
2. Start the meeting on time, even if some stragglers come late.
3. Provide a copy of the agenda.
4. Create common understanding at the outset. You should confirm that
   everyone understands:
   ✓ the purpose
   ✓ the amount of time that the meeting will take
   ✓ the process that will be used

5. Get organized. Since you will be preoccupied with the process and content, it is valuable to have others assist in different roles. For example, you may want to get volunteers to:
   ✓ keep time
   ✓ take the minutes
   ✓ record items on a flip chart, as needed
6. Keep the process moving, one item at a time. Each item may require a different process depending on whether it is:
   ✓ *Information Sharing*. This purpose often requires a formal presentation. It's good to have visuals so that members can see what is being discussed.
   ✓ *Feedback*. This agenda item requires that you give everyone a chance to comment on an issue. Encourage people to listen to each other's ideas, and record them on the flip chart if necessary. If there is concern that a few people will dominate the discussions, consider a round-robin approach—giving each person a chance to speak in turn—enabling people to "pass" if they have nothing new to contribute.
   ✓ *Problem Solving*. Take a systematic approach. Start with agreement about the nature of the problem. State it succinctly. Next, canvass for ideas as to the cause. If a variety of ideas are offered, consider recording these on the flip chart or with sticky notes. Group the ideas and discuss them until a consensus emerges as to which is/ are the most important. Finally, agree on a plan of action, making sure that someone takes responsibility for each item.
   ✓ *Planning*. Create a list of items that need to be taken care of and allocate responsibility for each item. Get commitment to a specific date for completion.
7. At the end of the meeting summarize what has been achieved and any plans for a follow-up meeting. Thank those who have attended.

If the meeting has not been as constructive as you would like, take a risk and share that observation with participants. Ask them for ideas as to what could be done better next time.

Mistakes: Turning Adversity into Opportunity

When one door of happiness closes, another opens; but often we look so long at the closed door that we do not see the one which has been opened for us.

—Helen Keller

Things do go wrong at work—lots of times, in fact. Hopefully things go well and according to plan most of the time. But how we deal with problems will set the tone for how employees behave. Dealing with mistakes effectively will improve morale, encourage accountability and responsibility, and promote innovation and calculated risk taking.

✓ Create a culture in which investigations of mistakes focus more on *what* went wrong rather than *who* went wrong.

✓ Look to learn from mistakes rather than to bury them. See mistakes as an opportunity to do better rather than as a lack of success.

✓ Analyze the culture of your organization to evaluate how mistakes are dealt with. Ask yourself:

• Do our managers deny problems in the hopes of avoiding embarrassment?

• Are my fellow senior managers willing to hear only good news?

• How do we deal with people who make mistakes? Are we harsh? Do we point fingers at them to the point where confidence is shattered? Or do we adopt an adult approach, focusing on the issue in the hope of finding the root cause of the problem and avoiding a repetition in the future?

- Do we offer rewards or recognition for those who take calculated risks to improve performance?

- How much backbone do middle managers show when dealing with challenging situations? Do they retreat into their "foxholes"? Or do they demonstrate courage and stand firm for ideas that they believe in?

- How difficult is it to go it alone and take a risk? Do our managers tend to go overboard to achieve widespread support (consensus) before taking a risk? And are they doing so because they are unwilling to take a chance on their own? Do they create mounds of paperwork, requiring sign-offs on the smallest details, in order to spread the blame?

- Do I obsess about even the most minor issues? Sweating the smallest stuff can be ruinous—the cost is high and the benefit small.

- Do we celebrate and make heroes of those who try—even if they fail? Do we recognize the initiative as worthy even if the result failed to meet expectations?

- Do I shirk leadership responsibility at the first sign of a setback? Or do I take responsibility, admit the error, revise the plan, and announce how improvements will be made? Do I involve those whose help I need to get back on track?

- Do I set realistic expectations when new initiatives are launched? Reasonable expectations will be less likely to produce recriminations when mistakes are made.

Mistakes: When Others Fail

A failure means you've put forth some effort. That's good. Failure gives you an opportunity to learn a better way to do it. That's positive. A failure teaches you something and adds to your experience. That's very helpful. Failure is an event, never a person; an attitude, not an outcome; a temporary inconvenience; a stepping stone. Our response to it determines just how helpful it can be.

— Zig Ziglar, legendary salesman

Mistakes are commonplace in organizations. Responses to mistakes can vary dramatically, from firing to empathy. Here is what to do when an employee makes a mistake:

- ✓ *Deal with it quickly*. Mistakes uncorrected send a message that they are acceptable.
- ✓ *Deal with the issue clinically*. If you have a tendency to become emotional about problems, calm down first and collect your thoughts as to how to respond in a professional manner.
- ✓ *Collect all the facts*. Get to the root cause of the problem. First, establish whether what happened *was* a mistake or just another way of dealing with the issue. Maybe the employee has found another way of doing things that could be equally good or even better. If not, take the next step.
- ✓ *Confront the issue, not the person*. Beating up on someone by using the "you" word will only intimidate him, causing him to lose self-confidence and make even more mistakes later on.

✓ *Treat the person with compassion*. Who has never made a mistake herself? Show understanding by listening and demonstrating empathy.

✓ *Turn the negative into a positive*. Make this a learning opportunity. If possible, get the employee to verbalize how she might deal with the issue differently next time.

✓ *Determine whether attitude or lack of training is a root cause*. If the issue is attitudinal, inform the employee of the consequence of further mistakes, asking for his commitment to do better next time. If the problem arose from a lack of training, ensure that this is rectified in an appropriate manner.

✓ *Follow up to ensure that the mistake does not recur*. Praise the employee for correcting the problem, or apply the appropriate consequences if she has not.

Planning

A good plan today is better than a perfect plan tomorrow.

—General George S. Patton

Examine the achievements of successful leaders in any field, and you'll find it all started with the pursuit of a goal or dream. But these people went beyond just thinking about their goals and dreams. They formulated a plan and put that plan into action.

With so many demands on our time and energy today, it makes sense to work from a plan. As a leader, planning is crucial to your ability to articulate goals to your team and guide them in the achievement of those goals. Here are strategies you and your employees can apply individually and jointly in order to plan effectively

1. Think on paper.
    ✓ Record all your ideas, whether you are brainstorming long-term plans with your team or simply putting together your to-do list for tomorrow. This is an essential first step for making any plan a reality.
    ✓ Work from a written plan. Find a system for formulating and tracking plans that works for you. Investigate planning tools such as Program Evaluation Review Technique (PERT) charts and Gantt charts. Some people like elaborate electronic systems, and others find old-fashioned pen and paper work best for them. Using a

system to visually record and track your plans will allow you to monitor your people's progress, identify potential problems, and make corrections as necessary.

2. Start with the long-term view and work backward. If you call a travel agency to book a trip, one of the first questions you will be asked is "What is your destination?" Similarly, to formulate a good plan for any purpose, you need to be clear about what you want to achieve.

   ✓ Develop the clearest goal statement you can. Identify concrete, measurable outcomes. For example, "improve unit productivity" is too vague and can't be measured. "Increase unit productivity by 20 percent by December 31" is clear and measurable.

   ✓ Break big plans down into the smallest steps. Write down every step that needs to be taken by you or others to achieve your plan. When your employees articulate goals that sound vague, push them to be as detailed as they can.

3. Identify the resources you will need.

   ✓ What do you or your people need to buy, borrow, or allocate? Look at the details formulated in step two to identify what will be needed at every phase. Remember that it's always a good idea to overestimate what you will need in terms of time or money.

   ✓ Consider who has the skills and talents that could help your plan to succeed. How much of their time will you need? (They might be in a better position to answer this question than you.) Will your employees need additional training or tools to help achieve this plan?

   ✓ Whose buy-in or support do you need? Who will be most affected by the implementation of your plan? Even if these stakeholders don't need to contribute any time or effort, getting their agreement to your plan may be essential to its long-term success. Ensure that your own manager is included in the approval process.

4. Acknowledge potential obstacles. It's easy to get caught up in the excitement of brainstorming and much less pleasant to think about

what can go wrong, but anticipating problems is an essential part of the planning process.

✓ Just as you might brainstorm ideas alone or with others, take time to generate a list of all the factors that could interfere with your plan. Be sure to solicit input from people who can anticipate obstacles you haven't thought of.

✓ Be realistic about obstacles that might seriously derail your plan. Don't minimize major concerns that could pose a serious impediment at a critical juncture.

✓ Listen carefully when your employees generate potential obstacles you haven't considered. Working on the front lines may give them a more realistic grasp of what could go wrong in the implementation phase.

✓ Take action on the obstacles that you can prevent or minimize. Ask others for help with the obstacles that you might not be able to handle yourself.

5. Continually clarify priorities and next steps.

✓ Start and finish each day with a clear focus. Pick two or three next steps on which you and your employees need to focus. Regularly ask yourself and your people, "How am I (or how are you) doing? What do I (you) need to do next?"

✓ Don't confuse activity with progress. You and your employees may seem very busy but it's important to ensure that everyone's efforts are actually making progress toward the desired goals. You can do this by holding regular check-in meetings and monitoring how your team members are spending their time on a day-to-day basis.

6. Make it easy to get started.

✓ Assemble the tools, equipment, and people you need. If you plan to exercise at your health club on the way home from work three days this week but your gym bag remains in your closet, it's unlikely that your plan will come to pass. If you put a fully stocked gym bag in your car, preferably next to the driver's seat where you can't miss it, you are much more likely to follow through. Similarly, to whatever extent you can, assemble what you need to take the next steps in your plan. Before you leave the office, put that phone number you need to call or that file you need to read front and center on your desk, where you will see it as soon as you arrive the next morning.

✓ Just get started. Other priorities will always be competing for your attention. Commit a specific amount of time to work on your plan, even if it's only thirty minutes, and treat that as a firm appointment in your schedule. Resolve to be single-minded in focusing on your plan during that time and don't allow anything, short of a serious emergency, to distract you. You may find that after thirty minutes you've built up enough momentum to keep going. If not, at least you've made a start.

7. Avoid procrastinating.

✓ Do the easiest thing first. If you feel stalled, pick the smallest, easiest step you can take and do it. If you can take enough of those small, easy steps, the remaining work that needs to be done may not seem so intimidating.

✓ Do the hardest thing first. An alternative strategy for beating procrastination is to tackle the most challenging aspect of your plan and get it out of the way first. Knowing that the hardest part is behind you can motivate you and your employees to push on and get the remaining, easier steps completed.

✓ Find out what's hindering your employees in getting started. If there seems to be a delay in getting things under way, talk with your team to find out where the roadblocks are.

8. Expect the unexpected. Despite your best efforts to anticipate obstacles, things can and will go wrong.

✓ See problems as a normal part of the implementation process. Bring your employees together, define the unexpected problem in clear terms, and then lead the team in brainstorming possible solutions.

✓ Be open to chance factors influencing your plans. Sudden changes in corporate goals, market trends, or other factors may require that a plan in progress be put on hold or even cancelled. It can be discouraging for you and your employees to have to halt or abandon a plan. If the project is being suspended just temporarily, explain the reasons why, when you expect that it can be restarted and what other tasks or projects will take priority for the time being.

✓ Don't be tempted to put off telling your employees if a plan must be cancelled. Explain the reasons for cancellation clearly and briefly. Acknowledge the hard work that's been done and the disappointment your employees may feel. Emphasize new skills they developed or new ideas the team generated that could be of use in the future. Then help the team to begin focusing on the next plan.

9. Assess your plan regularly. Whether you've made plans for your career, your team, your health, or your personal finances, set aside time regularly to evaluate your progress and direction.

✓ Choose regular intervals to assess existing plans and formulate new ones. You might organize an annual or semiannual team meeting to work on business goals, or plan a "meeting" with yourself at similar intervals to look at your individual goals, both business and personal.

✓ Don't assume that no news is good news. Even if all seems to be progressing as expected, don't be tempted to skip regular check-in meetings with your employees.

Problem Solving

The measure of success is not whether you have a tough problem to deal with but whether it's the same problem you had last year.

—John Foster Dulles

Problem solving starts with good intentions, because it often includes making ethical decisions. It is executed in a step-by-step process that ends in implemented actions. These are the steps to solving tough problems.

STEP 1: *UNDERSTAND THE PROBLEM*

Get a solid grip on the issues. Gather as much relevant information as is available to give you a good understanding of the situation from all perspectives. Make a list of all the stakeholders and their needs and expectations.

STEP 2: *DEFINE THE PROBLEM*

In a succinct statement, document the problem by describing:

✓ *who* was involved
✓ *what* happened
✓ *when* it took place
✓ *where* it happened
✓ *why* it occurred
✓ *how* it took place

STEP 3: CONSIDER YOUR VALUES

Reflect on the documented values of your organization as well as your own set of moral principles. Are there conflicts? Can a resolution be made that fits or is it likely to cut across values that either you or the organization hold sacred?

STEP 4: IDENTIFY THE ROOT CAUSE

List all the possible causes of the problem, then prioritize them based on facts and observations, before your instincts or gut feeling. Limit your list of root cause(s) to as few as possible.

STEP 5: CHOOSE A SOLUTION

Again, look for more than one solution before picking the best. The best solution should be the one that:

- ✓ is easiest to implement
- ✓ has the lowest cost
- ✓ satisfies as many stakeholders as possible
- ✓ is most compatible with your values

STEP 6: IMPLEMENT THE SOLUTION

Continue to monitor the situation to ensure that the problem has been resolved.

Professionalism

If you tell the truth you don't have to remember anything.

—Mark Twain

As a leader, you set the tone for others. Your behavior will be closely watched—and copied.

- ✓ Always be pleasant. It takes far fewer facial muscles to smile than to frown, so smile often. Make eye contact with people you meet.
- ✓ Greet people by name. Employees appreciate being recognized as individuals.
- ✓ Listen to others in meetings. Don't interrupt or cut people off. If they are going on much longer than they should, paraphrase back to them what you have understood to be their key messages.
- ✓ Always introduce others who are with you to people you bump into. It demonstrates that you value them.
- ✓ Never take anything for granted. Always say please and thank you.
- ✓ Avoid office gossip. If someone tells you a rumor, do not reply. Do not comment on the idea. Avoid basing evaluations on the information.
- ✓ Stay out of office politics. As difficult as this may be, avoid choosing sides in disputes that have little to do with issues and everything to do with personalities. Keep your eye on the ball: the goals you have set for yourself and those around you. Stop people in their tracks if they

want to tell you something in confidence, unless it has nothing to do with undermining someone else in the company.

✓ Dress for success and acceptance. Always dress one level better of what others might expect of you. Dressing down might appear humble but will project a poor image. Look the part that you want to be. Always be neat and tidy.

✓ Be timely in everything you do. Return phone calls and e-mails as quickly as possible. Be at a meeting on time or a bit before time to make sure that you are ready.

✓ Be willing to listen to others even if you think that your opinion will differ. Lean forward and show, with your body language and eye contact, that you are listening to them.

✓ Don't argue with people needlessly. Be tactful. Before you offer another suggestion, acknowledge their suggestions by summarizing them and then presenting your ideas, and ask for their opinions and support. Avoid using the "but" word before presenting an alternative.

✓ Always show interest in the people around you. If you're running short of time, apologize and offer to see people later.

✓ Encourage those lower in the corporate hierarchy to strive for im-provement. Share your strategies with them.

✓ Model the behavior you expect from others. Know, that as a leader, others are looking to you for cues about how they should act in similar circumstances.

Teamwork

A committee is a group that keeps minutes and loses hours.
—Milton Berle

Some people see working in a team-based organization as slow-moving and inefficient. If teamwork means collaboration, is there any alternative? Surely not. Knowing when to use a team to make decisions and when decisions should be made by a leader is important. It will help to build commitment when needed and speed up decisions when necessary.

✓ Effective team leaders know that not all decisions need to involve the team. In fact, the team would not be consulted when:
  • a decision needs to be made urgently
  • one member is an expert in the matter under consideration
  • the leader is specifically empowered to make the decision

✓ Team members should be involved in decisions that:
  • are complex
  • require a creative solution
  • need the commitment of the members to the outcome

✓ Team decisions should ideally be made as commonsense agreements that all the members can live with. They need not be thrilled with the outcome, but they should feel that it has sufficient merit to win their support.

✓ Working in a team is challenging. It's difficult enough to work effectively with one other person, and much more difficult to work with many, especially in view of the different personalities, perspectives, goals, and levels of motivation. To be successful requires that all members work hard to reap the rewards of their combined talents.

✓ Helping a disparate group of people to band together will be easier if you ensure that they incorporate these essential team elements in their daily activities:

- *Clear Goals and Objectives.* The goals should be specific, measurable, agreed upon, realistic (yet challenging), and time-based (SMART). The agreed-upon element is important in creating shared ownership.

- *Shared Rewards and Benefits.* The "what's in it for us" syndrome finds meaning for members if benefits are linked to performance and goal achievement. The rewards could be tangible—such as shared bonuses—but should also include nonmonetary rewards such as accolades from the CEO or board, celebratory parties, pizza lunches, or outings together.

- *Well-Defined Structure and Roles.* The team needs to divide roles so that everyone knows how to work together without stepping on each other's toes. Roles should also be clearly defined so that leadership is a nonissue. Someone needs to take ultimate responsibility for keeping the team on track.

- *Agreed-Upon Ground Rules.* The team members should define the quality of their relationships with one another, including decision-making processes, in terms of open communications, trust, support, and loyalty.

- *Standards of Performance.* The team needs to identify its customers (internal or external) and how it intends to serve them. What minimum level of performance is acceptable? How quickly should each key activity be executed? How does the team measure success, and what should be the minimum level of achievement?

- *Clear Communication.* No matter who makes the decisions, the entire team must know what is going on. Keep the team up-to-date as a group; don't breed dissatisfaction by encouraging or engaging in piecemeal, one-on-one information sharing.

✓ Make changes to the team when necessary. One bad apple can have a major debilitating impact on the team, and this situation is sometimes allowed to continue for years. A decisive leader who fails to turn nonperformers around will be lauded for decisive action in removing people whose values are incompatible with those of the team. Their departures can boost morale tremendously. And equally important is that this action sends a strong signal about the leader's values and priorities.

Technology

Everything that can be invented, has been invented.
—Charles H. Duell, 1899

If you feel that the technological developments you've recently experienced are impressive, for sure you're going to be even more amazed in the years ahead. Astonishing advances not even contemplated a few years ago are now just around the corner. Consider, for example, that in the eight months between the time that these words are written and then published, the number of transistors in a microprocessor may double to almost a billion. When the first microprocessor was created in 1971, it contained 2,250 transistors. And every eighteen months since then the numbers have doubled.

These developments will change our lives in many ways as these microscopic chips find their way into all facets of our lives. No other aspect of our organizations changes as quickly as information technology (IT), which makes that aspect difficult to understand and control. As a leader you cannot afford to spend time being the technical guru, but you can ensure that technology helps add value to your organization's success. These practices will make that a reality:

- ✓ Demonstrate the importance of technology as a key ingredient for survival and growth by working closely with your chief technology officer and her staff.
- ✓ To identify new opportunities to improve, benchmark your IT practices against organizations that have excellent reputations in the IT field.

In order to identify what levels of service are reasonable and practical, listen to companies that want you to outsource your IT function to them. Hold your IT department to the same service standards as may be available from outside.

✓ Evaluate who is doing the value-added tasks—your own employees or consultants. It is a generally accepted principle that anything created by your own employees remains the property of the company. However, in general, anything created by external consultants belongs to them and can be used outside your organization unless it is specifically agreed to the contrary in writing.

✓ Review work that is done in-house that could potentially be outsourced. Conversely, are there opportunities to "in-source" work that could be done more effectively by your own employees and give you the additional benefit of flexibility and control? If outsourcing is an option, consider the problems that must be overcome, including:
  • lack of control
  • lack of flexibility
  • redundancy among employees and its impact on morale
  • the cost of employee severances

✓ Be sensitive to the number of platforms being used across the organization, with a view to standardizing. Consult with your IT people to ensure that your platforms are compatible with those being used in the organizations to ensure standardization and compatibility wherever possible.

✓ Encourage your staff to follow personal-use policies so that everyone knows:
  • how much time, if any, can be devoted to personal surfing and e-mails
  • the types of Web sites or specific sites that are either approved or forbidden for access
  • the types of messages from outside the organization that employees

are strictly forbidden to distribute, such as jokes, sexist materials, chain letters, and pornography

✓ The form of disciplinary action associated with infractions should also be specified. How this policy will be enforced will be influenced by factors such as the cost of policing and the severity and sensitivity of each breach of company policy.

✓ Review the strategy and costs associated with avoiding spam and viruses, such as the use of specific software and firewalls. Look for new and productive ways to deal with this scourge.

✓ Review the practicality of the technology being used. Is it the most practical or is it the most fashionable—and possibly the most expensive? Ask yourself if less-expensive systems might do the job equally well.

✓ Evaluate the policy on funding new equipment. Are you taking advantage of group discounts? Are you getting the best tax advantages from purchasing practices? Are you leasing equipment that has a short life span and buying equipment that has a longer life span?

Ten Traits of Great Leaders

My grandfather, Eyes-that-Sparkle, told our tribe, "Never cross a river until you come to it." But in my generation, the world is owned by those who have made the crossing in their imagination far ahead of the crowd.

—Grey Owl (Archibald Belaney)

Leaders attract people to follow them. They have perfected the art of getting others to do something because they—the followers—want to do it. Much has been written on how leaders do this. In all the research and observations it appears that ten traits separate great leaders from their peers.

1. *Ability to Create a Compelling Vision.* Leaders focus on the future. They have a clear picture of what they want the organization to become. They are excited about the future and don't waste time dealing with the past.

2. *Ability to Articulate Their Vision to Others.* Leaders have an ability to describe that future state in words and feelings that captivate and galvanize those around them. They constantly share their views of the world with those who look to them for guidance.

3. *Consistency.* Great leaders don't change with the wind. They are flexible and open to new ideas, but they tend to be constant in their beliefs and values. Once they have articulated their visions, they keep on track without getting distracted by competing temptations. They tend not to buy in to the "flavor of the month" program only to chop and change at the slightest sign of a roadblock.

4. *Humility.* High achievers have justifiable pride in their accomplishments. Leaders are human—they make mistakes. But they are not afraid to admit it when they go wrong. They are good listeners. They are as interested as learning from others as they are in sharing their own thoughts. Humble people also appreciate feedback. They thrive on learning when they've done well. And they're interested in learning from their mistakes so that they can do better.

5. *Focus.* Leaders focus on key results. They are not distracted by trivia. Whatever they do, they complete with excellence.

6. *Tenacity.* Leaders anticipate problems and work diligently until they overcome obstacles.

7. *Holistic Thinking.* Leaders can see the big picture as well as the interrelationship among the parts.

8. *Strategic Thinking.* Leaders have an eye on the future. They spend little time thinking about the "good old days." They have a clear sense of what they should do to anticipate and meet future challenges.

9. *Agile Minds.* Leaders learn quickly. They observe everything around them and ask lots of questions so that they can become more proficient in their knowledge and skills. They are adaptable. Future leaders can modify their behavior to find quick acceptance from people in a variety of situations and with people at all levels of an organization.

10. *Aversion to Tyranny.* Leaders are fair-minded and avoid taking abusive advantage of people and situations.

PART 2

Life and Career Management

> Staying young is mostly brought about by ensuring that
> your dreams far outnumber your regrets.
>
> —Grey Owl (Archibald Belaney)

Effective leaders are multifaceted. They have an eye on the present and they have an eye on tomorrow. They look out for their people but they take care of themselves too. Their careers are not the only focus of their daily activities, but their actions ensure that their positions are both secure and enhanced. But they need to do more; they need to be proactive in making sure that their efforts, energy, and contributions are reflected in their success and their status in their organizations. Chapters 20 through 27 will help leaders reach the top of their organizations—and stay at the top.

Balancing Your Life

The problem with the rat race is that even if you win, you're still a rat.

—Lily Tomlin

Health experts emphasize the importance of living a balanced lifestyle, yet stress-related illnesses and workplace absenteeism rates continue to skyrocket. There's no doubt that our society—and many companies—encourage a hard-driving, almost obsessive commitment to work. But is this really the best approach?

You have probably heard of (and perhaps even know) people who have transformed their lives after experiencing a wake-up call in the form of a health crisis. These people often make drastic changes, moving into a new career or a different place of residence, exercising and enjoying leisure activities more frequently, and examining every aspect of their lives to create a better balance. Why wait until a crisis forces you to make these kinds of changes? A balanced life includes a healthy blend of work, play, and rest. Only you can decide what constitutes a good mix for you.

Maintaining a balanced life is important for everyone, but it's essential for those in leadership roles. As a leader, you deal with more intense pressures and shoulder more responsibilities than the average worker. You likely set the pace of work for many other people, either by example or through delegation. Being in a position of influence gives you an opportunity to show others that it is possible to be successful and productive without sacrificing your health, your relationships, or your happiness. Here's how to create a more balanced lifestyle for yourself and those around you.

✓ Be a role model.

- Examine your own lifestyle. Do you take pride in being "on" and ready to work 24/7? It's likely that your employees, your peers, and even your family feel a lot of pressure to keep up. Pushing yourself (and others) relentlessly to produce around the clock may seem feasible and may even yield productivity gains in the short term. Often the negative effects of this kind of work pace aren't seen until after many years, when the long-term strain on your body begins to create health problems. You do no one any favors if you drive yourself into a hospital bed or an early grave. Ask yourself if you would want your best friend or your children to emulate your approach to balancing life.

- Identify areas where better balance is needed in your life. Perhaps you get a sufficient amount of exercise and sleep, but your diet is poor or you don't spend enough time with your family. Don't try to make sweeping changes overnight. Pick one or two small changes that you can live with for now, such as resolving to leave work promptly at five p.m. one night a week (unless there is a serious emergency that simply can't wait until the next morning). Plan an activity you really enjoy for that evening so you will be more likely to leave promptly. Once that change has become a permanent part of your life, pick another small step to take toward a more balanced life.

- Deal with stress before it builds to an unhealthy level. A certain amount of stress is good for us. It makes us stronger, helps us to be resilient, and is often the driving force for making improvements in our lives. But too much stress places a burden on your body and mind. Watch for signs that you are starting to feel the effects of stress. For example, some people start to have trouble sleeping or overreact to minor irritations. Take steps to relieve the pressure before it gets worse.

✓ Pay attention to how your employees are balancing *their* lives. A burned-out worker who has to take an extended stress leave is of no value to you. It is expensive to be constantly replacing good workers who must leave your team because they find that the job demands too many sacrifices in their personal lives.

- Ensure that your employees take regular vacations and use all of their allotted vacation time. Put systems in place so workers won't feel so indispensable that they can't take time away from the office to rest and recharge.

- Monitor their workloads. Ensure that workers share the load fairly. Take steps to get assistance for workers who are struggling with an unrealistic burden of tasks and projects.

- Look for opportunities to implement workplace programs that help to reduce workers' stress (and your own) and contribute to better life balance. Flexible hours, telecommuting, on-site day care, and fitness facilities are just a few examples of workplace initiatives that have reduced absenteeism in many companies.

- Encourage regular hours. It's wonderful to be blessed with workers who are so committed to their jobs that they willingly put in overtime. But a workplace culture that demands that workers constantly sacrifice their personal lives is likely to lead to a burned-out, less productive team in the long run. Although there may be periods where overtime is necessary, ensure that your employees take sufficient time off to compensate and understand that you don't expect them to make a habit of working excessive hours.

✓ View rest as a joy, not a necessary evil.

- If you think that sleep is a waste of time and recreation is only for the lazy or weakhearted, adjust your mindset. You stop to fill your gas tank and have routine maintenance done on your car before it breaks down. Why not give yourself the same attention? After you have worked a certain number of hours without a break, your productivity begins to drop. Pushing yourself to work beyond that threshold means that the law of diminishing returns begins to take effect. It may take you twice as long to get the same amount of work done as if you were rested. If nothing else, consider your efforts to balance your life as better for your long-term performance and productivity than driving yourself through long periods without any respite.

- Take all of your allotted vacation. Workers in the United States and Canada have a lower allocation of vacation time than in many other countries. In spite of this, many people don't take all of the vacation days available to them each year. If it's simply impossible for you to be spared for any significant length of time, consider spreading out your vacation days to take a series of long weekends. You may find them just as restful as taking all your time in one block. Or add a few days on to a business trip and have your family join you.

- Get all the sleep you need. Many people walk around chronically sleep deprived, without realizing the effect their fatigue has on their performance. If you find yourself fighting the urge to doze off during meetings, on commuter trains, or even at the wheel of your car, it's likely you're not getting enough rest. Assuming that you don't suffer from a sleeping disorder or a condition that causes fatigue, the obvious answer to this problem is simply to get more sleep. Examine how you spend your evening hours and consider what you could do to make more time available for sleep. Make the last hour before bed your time to wind down. Avoid doing any work or physical activity. Resist the urge to check the news channel for the latest headlines or stock market reports. Increase the amount of time that you sleep in fifteen- to thirty-minute increments until you wake up feeling rested in the morning and don't experience any drowsiness during the day.

✓ Make time away count for both you and your employees.

- Leave your cell phone or pager turned off and resolve not to check your e-mail during weekends and vacations—unless there is a situation you simply must monitor. If you can't afford to be that disconnected, designate a specific time of day for checking in, then stay unplugged and disconnected the rest of the time. If you're in the habit of working through your entire weekend, declare at least a few hours a work-free period.

• Discourage your employees from checking in during vacation. A surprising number of people check voice mail and e-mail during vacation, even though their managers don't expect them to. Encourage your employees to keep things covered during each other's absence so they don't need to worry about their responsibilities while away.

✓ Cultivate relaxing hobbies to offset your busy lifestyle.

• Try a noncompetitive hobby. Golfing with clients to close business deals or playing a hard-hitting game of squash with a colleague may provide some fitness benefits, but these activities are unlikely to leave you feeling relaxed. Choose an enjoyable activity or hobby that has no competitive quality and encourages a slower pace. Tai chi, gardening, hiking, and bird watching are just a few examples of hobbies that can give you an opportunity to relax without having to focus on winning or reaching a specific goal.

• Learn to relax deeply. If you have a stressful lifestyle and work at a frenetic speed most of the time, it is even more vital that you balance your usual pace with deep relaxation. The ability to relax deeply—which is different from sleeping or engaging in quiet recreation—is often cultivated through meditation, deep breathing, or activities like yoga. A few minutes of deep relaxation can leave you as rested as if you'd had many hours of sleep.

✓ Maximize your days to ensure that you have as much leisure time as possible. Do so by:

• Getting as much done as you can while traveling. A person can do much uninterrupted work on an airplane or a train.

• Using meal times for meetings that are difficult to schedule during normal working hours. Ensure that you immediately identify the purpose of the meeting and that most of the conversation focuses on that issue.

✓ Take a monthly time-out: a day off in a place where you cannot be disturbed and where your thinking can predominate. A public or university library is a wonderful example. Using the biggest desk you can find, spread out all your tasks on the table, creating piles of paper ordered by project and priority. Take the time to do things you have neglected—for example, writing thank-you notes or messages of congratulations. Coming back to work with a clean slate will make you feel great, and your confidence will radiate to those around you.

✓ Treat your family like a key client. This will encourage you to set aside more quality time with them, and they will be more likely to support you when you need to be away and focused on your job. When you're at home, set aside time for talking. Make sure that the TV is off and that no reading material is around that might distract you. Be sure to look at your family members when they talk to you, and summarize back to them what you have heard.

Career Development

The way I see it, if you want the rainbow, you gotta put up with the rain.

—Dolly Parton

Research indicates that career executives are spending less time than ever in jobs before moving on to better opportunities. This creates many more new opportunities than ever before. You always need to be ready to make the next move or to be invited to undertake a more advanced, high-profile challenge.

Taking care of the shareholders, customers, and employees is important, but you are still number one. Every leader needs to set aside time for his or her own development. You must be able to land on your feet if your career suddenly hits a roadblock—or a superhighway.

- ✓ Stay in line management—that's where the action is! Line managers are in the limelight. They produce the crucial results in sales and production. Staff positions are important, but they serve the people who serve the key stakeholders—the customers.
- ✓ Take responsibility for your career. Don't expect your boss to campaign for you or promote you. *You* need to plan your career path, determine the knowledge and level of performance that will take you there, and acquire and demonstrate those key leadership skills.
- ✓ Set goals for yourself. Decide where you'd like to be three, five, and ten years from now. Make a list of obstacles that might prevent you from achieving those goals. Then identify the roadblocks and what you

can do to remove them. Don't get overwhelmed if the obstacles look daunting. Develop plans to systematically remove them, one at a time, over time.

✓ Be your customers' best friend. Your customers are key stakeholders and they, more than anyone, will sell your skills to the top decision makers. So identify the highest-profile customers and do everything you can to ensure that they sing your praises.

✓ Think strategically about the future of your organization and your career. Take time to do this at least monthly, as circumstances can change quickly. Consider new developments in your organization and in your current industry. How will these affect you? What opportunities do they create? What challenges do they present?

✓ Become your own greatest advocate. Look at yourself as a client who needs PR. Make yourself known. Make sure that people in your industry know of you and your accomplishments. At corporate and industry gatherings, stay around so that you can network, looking particularly for the movers and shakers who can influence your career.

✓ Be ready to take advantage of new opportunities when they occur. They will probably happen when you least expect it. Realize that the job you have will not last forever. Chances are that, sooner or later, you will be offered a promotion or the job of your dreams—or possibly be given an awkward handshake and asked to leave right away.

✓ Take care of yourself. Keep your mind and body in good shape. Keeping fit will make you feel good, look good, and act enthusiastically and with confidence. And if you smoke, make the extra effort to kick the habit.

✓ Treat everyone with respect. Never do anything that could embarrass a peer or a boss or a member of the board. Deal with disagreements in private. If you need to challenge someone, ensure that you focus on the issue and not the person. Recognize that their positions are legitimate, even though you see things differently.

✓ Develop alliances. Identify people who might want to hold you back, and be careful not to offend them. Better still, ensure good relations with *their* subordinates. If someone belittles you behind your back, others will speak up in your defense and the person who is showing no class will harm his own reputation as a consequence.

✓ Be nice to people. Get to know as many of your colleagues as possible by first name. When you have time, practice management by walking around. In fact, make a point of setting aside time to get as friendly with as many people as possible.

✓ Go the extra mile. Be a little better than your peers. Come early to meetings. Stay an extra five minutes before taking lunch or going home. Put in extra time when a situation demands it—without sacrificing too much family time.

✓ Don't take work home. If necessary, close your door to make sure that you focus and clean your desk before going home. A healthy and happy home life will enable you to be positive and enthusiastic at work.

✓ Take a leadership role in the most important and visible projects. Focus on them and make sure that they are completed on time and on budget.

✓ Be obliging, especially if the CEO or your board has a request. This will earn you a "can-do" reputation, which will position you well for promotion.

✓ Bosses hate surprises! They like advance notice of new initiatives that will require some thought before action is needed. If one of your projects is going off the rails, let your boss know as soon as possible— before he hears the bad news through the grapevine.

✓ Make your boss look good, especially if she is the president! This will pay huge dividends sooner or later. And if you can, make your boss's boss look even better; that person will have even more influence over your career. Why? Your boss may feel threatened by the possibility of your replacing her, but your boss's boss certainly won't.

✓ If you are frustrated with your role in the organization, consider the fit between your skills and your job. Would other roles suit you better and allow you to shine? If so, here's what to do:

- Inform your boss of your frustration.
- If she agrees that a new direction would benefit both you and the organization, then the ball is in your court.
- Do everything you can to learn more about that new job, particularly the skill set necessary to be successful in it.
- Volunteer for task forces that concern the area of interest to you. This will give you exposure to people in that area and a better opportunity to understand the issues in more detail.

✓ Take every opportunity to learn. Learn from your mistakes, from reading, from a mentor, by listening intently to others, and by taking training courses. Research new ideas and share them with others too, because nothing will help you internalize new ideas better than teaching others.

Learning and Self-Development

I find television very educational. Every time someone switches it on,
I go into another room and read a good book.

—Groucho Marx

Being a lifelong learner is good for two reasons. First, you become a good role model for those around you, and second, your ability to take advantage of new, challenging opportunities will be enhanced. A variety of strategies can enhance your knowledge and skills.

✓ Identify your learning style. Then find opportunities that best fits the style you are most comfortable with. For example, consider these questions:
  • What learning opportunities in the past did you most enjoy? What did you least enjoy? Why?
  • Do you prefer to learn on your own or do you prefer team learning?
  • Do you like to be prepared before a formal learning session or do you enjoy the challenge of "winging it" during the session?
  • Do you like to have someone to facilitate your learning, providing you with a step-by-step process? Or do you prefer to figure things out for yourself?

✓ Find the learning opportunities that suit your learning style best. These could include:

- classroom/in-house sessions
- public workshops
- university executive programs
- an executive coach for regular one-on-one meetings
- computer-based training
- online learning
- personal research
- reading

✓ Take on at least one significant challenge each year. This could be work or pleasure. For example, learn to cook Mongolian food, master a new computer program, or become proficient in repairing appliances.

✓ Read journals, magazines, and books on management and related subjects. If this is too time-consuming, consider these strategies:
  - Buy tapes to listen to in your car or while traveling.
  - Get your employees to read periodicals and books and summarize the best ideas at a monthly lunch-and-learn session.

✓ Learn from your mistakes. Keep a journal of all the things you believe you did poorly or might have done better. Figure out how you might have treated an employee better, why you lost a client, why you were looked over for a promotion. Seek the answer within yourself and, if necessary, from a trusted friend.

✓ Find a coach. Many senior managers are turning for new wisdom and perspectives to seasoned professionals who may have traveled down the same or a similar path. Someone outside your organization can act as a sounding board for you when you're struggling to deal with new roadblocks. A good coach will listen to you and ask you questions that will help you discover your own answers. Having many and varied experiences in their pasts, coaches may also be able to share those experiences, helping you to find solutions that might fit your circumstances.

Learning: Strategies for Senior Executives

Only the curious will learn and only the resolute overcome the obstacles to learning. The quest quotient has always excited me more than the intelligence quotient.

—Eugene S. Wilson

Most executives not only have a solid formal education, they have also continued to learn at every opportunity. This learning has come about from formal skills development acquired at public courses, in-house programs, conferences, and, most importantly, by learning from mistakes!

Many of these formal learning opportunities diminish in value as you scale the corporate ladder. The number of programs available for executives is limited compared to the enormous quantity of programs for middle managers. However, the need to learn doesn't diminish as you move toward the top. But the type of learning changes, as does the process. The content of new learning will be more strategic, and the process must be more engaging. So here are some alternative choices for the executive of today.

✓ Find a coach.

Business coaches are appearing everywhere. Unfortunately, many human resources and other professionals get into this business as a way of sus-

taining themselves between jobs, and therefore are often ill-equipped to
be effective coaches. An effective coach will:
- have a demonstrated track record of success
- have certification from a recognized body
- be as interested in learning from you as you are from her
- be a good listener
- have been successful at overcoming some of the challenges you are
  faced with or have helped someone else with similar issues
- be available at a time and place convenient for you

✓ Join peer networking groups.

There are many opportunities to meet with peers in network groups, such as:
- *Young Presidents' Organization (YPO)*. YPO is a worldwide orga-
  nization open to people who meet the following criteria:
  - They are under the age of 45 at time of joining.
  - They hold the title of president, chairman of the board, chief
    executive officer, managing director, managing partner, or pub-
    lisher or the equivalent of any of these positions. A chairman of
    the board/chief executive officer and a president of the same com-
    pany may not simultaneously be members.
  - They employ at least fifty full-time people or pay salaries, exclud-
    ing the member's, of at least $1 million.
  - Their companies meet minimum annual revenue requirements or
    have an enterprise value of $10 million as defined by the net
    worth of assets before depreciation, an independent third-party
    investment/valuation, or the company's public equity value plus
    its debt, less cash.
- *Formal Networking Clubs*. These clubs are most often franchises
  run by well-connected local businesspeople. Membership is usually
  limited to a dozen executives, none of whom are from competing
  businesses. The members usually meet monthly, with each person
  getting the chance to host a session, thereby giving others an oppor-

tunity to learn about a new business. Members share their concerns in a confidential forum, allowing for input from others that may shed new light on a vexing problem. By offering advice to one another, these executives are often able to reflect on their own short-comings, as often there is a gap between what we know is right and what we actually do. These clubs also bring in high-caliber speakers who will challenge members with new ideas.

✓ Learn on the job.

Perfection eludes us all. We often fail to do things properly. But how often do we pause to reflect on the issue, figure out what we did wrong and how we might deal with it differently the next time? Opportunities to improve yourself are considerable. So take the time after every unsuccessful meeting, futile attempt at problem resolution, miscommunication with a colleague, or failure to meet your customer's needs, and figure out the problem. Take personal responsibility for fixing the problem by doing things better next time.

✓ Become a mentor.

That's right—don't find a mentor (not a bad idea either) but become one! How does mentorship help you learn? The best programs give senior managers an opportunity to mentor some of the best and brightest potential stars in the organization, often people with different technical backgrounds. This gives the mentor a wonderful chance to learn by exchanging information. And helping someone else grow enables you to develop yourself as well.

✓ Attend targeted executive education opportunities.

Set aside at least five days for your own personal education each year. Talk to others who have done likewise and see what kinds of opportunities exist. Keep changing how you do it, switching from a formal process to a less-formal one in the next program you take. Focus on opportunities that will stretch you and force you to operate outside your comfort zone.

✓ Be receptive to feedback—from your employees.

At least twice a year, absent yourself from departmental meetings and ask your employees to discuss your performance. One or two representatives can then summarize the discussion and provide you with key points on your strengths and areas that need development.

Life: Living Each Moment to the Fullest

Life is not measured by the number of breaths we take,
but by the moments that take our breath away.

—George Carlin

Our lives are not a dress rehearsal for something else. This is the real thing, the only chance we get to make the most of our lives. We can never know when the final moment of our lives may occur. So, we need to take every opportunity to make each day count as if it were our last.

✓ Ignore the numbers that never help you or cause you stress. These include age, height, or earnings.
✓ Surround yourself with people who are happy, smile often, and always see the glass as half full. Let go of the complainers.
✓ Keep learning. Learn in formal situations and learn from your mistakes. Seek out people who have complementary skills and ideas. Learn from them. Learn more about computers, crafts, gardening, whatever may interest you. Never let the brain idle.
✓ Enjoy the simple things. Learn to smell the roses.
✓ Laugh often, and with gusto. Never feel embarrassed to laugh out loud—it's often infectious. Laugh until you feel as if your body's going to explode. It won't.
✓ Deal with grief as a necessary but passing phase that cannot be

avoided. But don't get stuck in it. Life is too short. Honor those who have passed and care for those who are unwell. But move on—don't get stuck with things you have no control over. Treat your tears as a way to help you wash the sadness away. Enjoy the sense of relief and move on.

✓ Fill your life with love. Surround yourself with people you love and who love you in return. Listen to music that you love, over and over, till it stops giving you enjoyment. Keep near you pictures of the people and things that you love so that you can see them often.

✓ Cherish your health. If it is good, preserve it. If it is unstable, improve it. If it is beyond anything you can do to improve, get help.

✓ Avoid feeling guilty. Treat yourself to things that give you pleasure. Have the occasional piece of chocolate or your favorite full-fat ice cream. And (within reason) buy that luxury item you've always wanted. Savor these times of indulgence, but don't rely on them too often to make you happy.

✓ Tell the people you love that you love them—often.

Replacing Yourself

The best way to motivate other people to help you
fulfill your goals is to help them fulfill their goals.

—Deepak Chopra

You can't get promoted if you can't be replaced. This is a significant challenge today, as many organizations have downsized to the point where employees are working to full capacity, with little time left for their own development. So the pool of potential replacements is shallow indeed, requiring that we promote people because of their potential rather than their abilities. Here are some ideas to ensure that you are ready to move up the ladder when the call comes.

- ✓ See yourself as a coach. Make it your business to identify one or two key people for development and create a plan to enable them to step into your shoes at any time.
- ✓ Review the skills that made you successful—organizational, technical, and "soft" skills. Evaluate potential replacements and identify gaps in their knowledge. Let them know about your intention to develop them as your backup—it will be highly motivating for them.
- ✓ Identify your replacement's learning style. Some people are more self-directed while others prefer more structure, help, and guidance as they learn. Those that are more self-directed are able to take responsibility for their careers and learning and are probably going to be better replacements. Prioritize topics with the protégé and develop a list of learning opportunities (conferences, workshops, reading, and assignments, to name a few) that will be implemented over a reasonable period of time.
- ✓ Encourage retention of new skills by setting goals before each learning

opportunity. Equally important, follow up to find out how effective the training was, what was learned, and what new skills or behavior you are likely to notice. Reinforce the learning as often as you can; for learning to be internalized, it probably needs to be reinforced five to six times.

✓ Challenge your protégé with work assignments. On-the-job learning can be powerful. Ensure that each assignment has four phases:

- *Planning.* Identify the goals of the assignment. Next specify what steps (actions) are expected and what the final outcome will be (deliverables). Involve the protégé in the plan to ensure that she buys into the goals you are setting.

- *Action.* Allow the protégé to carry out the project. Monitor her progress, offering encouragement along the way. Note how she deals with adversity. Does she look to you for help when she encounters a roadblock or does she find a way to overcome the obstacle? Identify key points along the way to evaluate progress so that she can get feedback.

- *Evaluation.* Make notes on your observations so that you can be specific in your feedback. Also, if possible, measure progress so that your feedback will be accurate rather than general. Having pointed out any shortcomings that you might have observed, get your protégé's agreement to the facts presented. Then ask her to suggest new strategies to deal with the situation. You should suggest solutions only if she has no idea how to deal with the situation in the future (which is highly unlikely).

- *Revision.* Create a new plan for learning something new or set up a similar project to perfect your protégé's learning.

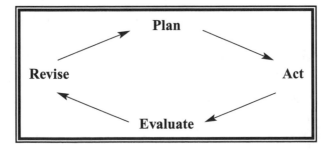

Setbacks: Overcoming Adversity in Your Career

> I think everyone should experience defeat at least once
> during their career. You learn a lot from it.
> —Lou Holtz, College Football Coach

Life is tough. The road is never just downhill, and there are bound to be many potholes that will throw you off course. But the blow need not be fatal. In fact, it can be beneficial and character building, especially if dealt with positively. So if a major project you've worked on is cancelled, your recommendations have been declined, or you've been overlooked for that promotion you were sure was a slam dunk, consider these strategies.

- ✓ Deal with your disappointment and anger in a place and manner that will ensure it doesn't come back to haunt you. If necessary, make an excuse to leave the premises so that you won't feel as if you're under the spotlight.
- ✓ Take a long walk so that you have time to cool your jets.
- ✓ Consider the reasons for your disappointment. Could you have done things differently? As hard as it is to be objective, can you think of causes for the problem? If you could rewind the life tape, could you have done things differently?
- ✓ Turn the negative into a positive. Identify the person(s) who might have been instrumental in delivering the blow and ask them for their

help and advice so that you don't get into the same situation again. Listen to their advice. Don't show anger or defensiveness. Write the advice down and summarize it at the end of your conversation.

✓ Make it your business never to make the same mistake again. At the same time, recognize that you are only human, and humans are fallible and will make many mistakes over a lifetime.

✓ One of the biggest life crises is getting fired—for just cause or not. Most people who have suffered this indignity recover from the stress (both mental and monetary) and end up happier than before. But the journey is often a tortuous one, even though it has become quite commonplace. So here are some ways to deal with the situation:

- Don't ignore your anger. Deal with it. And find a productive way to deal with it, since your frustration will show in your dealings with everyone you come in contact with. Find a way to ventilate: tell everyone you know, yell in the shower, or write a letter to the people who fired you and tell them how you feel—then tear up the letter.

- Make a new start. Turn the page and think out all the possibilities that await you. Dream about the job you've always wanted and then put a plan together to make it happen.

- Devote a set amount of time each day to your job search. This will give you a routine. Then balance your day with fun things that will keep you mentally and physically active. Don't put those fun things off till you get a job. Lying on the couch watching TV does not count! Take up yoga. Learn to paint or cook. Start exercising. Buy a bike and rediscover your city from a new perspective.

- Avoid the strategies used by most other people in your position, such as answering ads in the paper and sending résumés by e-mail.

- The best way to find that ideal job is through networking. Go through your list of contacts and separate them into "A," "B," and "C" categories. "A" people are senior organization people who are influential in the field that excites you. "B" people are good contacts but are unlikely to be of direct help in your area of interest. "C" people are people who may care about your career but are unlikely to be as influential or knowledgeable as you would like. Start with the "A"s, asking them not for a job but for their advice. Ask as many open-ended questions as time will permit. Try to see the "A" people face-to-face rather than discuss your search on the phone. The more time you spend with these people, the more likely they are to have a lead or other ideas for you. Follow up with a thank-you letter and a copy of your résumé.

✓ Listen carefully to everyone who offers advice. You may discover opportunities that can be fashioned into a job that doesn't yet exist. In such a case, ask for permission to present a proposal that could add value to the prospective employer's organization. Make sure that your presentation is well thought out, thoroughly researched, logical, positive, and documented. It will carry far more weight than a verbal sales pitch.

Values: A Personal Approach

I was, and am, a strong believer that one of the most satisfying things in life is to create a highly moral and ethical environment in which every individual is allowed and encouraged to realize their God-given potential.

—Jeff Skilling, Former Enron executive

I wonder how you feel about the above quotation from Jeff Skilling about ethical behavior. I won't comment, but I can anticipate your response. Words are empty without actions and behaviors to match. Research by James Kouzes and Barry Posner, documented in their book *Credibility: How Leaders Gain and Lose It, Why People Demand It*, suggested that honesty is the most frequently cited trait of a good leader.

Keeping your word and being true to ethical values is key. Astonishingly, many people who have been indicted for criminal behavior—particularly white-collar crimes—were often actively involved in their communities' charitable endeavors. How can this be? Is it possible to separate business ethics and personal values? Apparently so, but this cannot be good. So here is a guide to behaviors that will keep you out of trouble, let you sleep well at night, and be a great role model to those reporting to you.

The Ten Commandments, which mirror the basic values of all civilizations, deal explicitly with integrity, stating "Thou shalt not steal; thou shalt not kill; thou shalt not covet thy neighbor's house (or anything belonging to thy neighbor); and thou shalt not bear false witness against thy neighbor." Here are some benchmarks by which we can judge our own personal ethical behavior:

Rule 1   *Be honest.* Be truthful at all times, even when it hurts.

Rule 2   *Behave with integrity.* Demonstrate consistency in intention, word, and behavior.

Rule 3   *Take responsibility.* Ethical people learn to live with the consequences of their actions, whether intentional or unintentional.

Rule 4   *Respect the law.* As a citizen of your country, you should obey its laws, especially when they are based on democratic principles that intend freedom and equality for all citizens. In some countries this principle may challenge us, especially if the laws conflict with our ethical values.

Rule 5   *Be loyal.* Commit to serving and assisting the people with whom you choose to spend most of your time, including family, community, and work colleagues. You can also be loyal to your traditions while respecting those of others and being open to changing those that may fly in the face of human dignity.

Rule 6   *Work for a better world.* Go beyond a simple belief in the possibility of a better world. Choose your area of interest and work conscientiously to improve the lot of those in need. Contributing to better social, economic, and environmental conditions starts with those around you but can soon extend beyond.

Rule 7   *Be charitable.* This rule follows Rule 6. Most religions have some guidelines for giving.

Rule 8   *Be compassionate.* Give of your time to help others, conducting yourself with a sense of joy that you have been blessed more than so many others. Behave also with kindness and humility—always be ready to listen and offer advice and assistance.

Rule 9   *Be consistent.* Follow your principles all the time, with all your col-
           leagues. Don't play favorites. Don't change the rules because it appears
           to be expedient in the short run.

Rule 10   *Observe rules 1–9.*

PART 3

Strategic Leadership

The old shall have dreams and the youth shall have visions . . .
—Joel 3:1

Leaders are concerned about performance. They view the world as their stage and ensure that their plays please all the stakeholders. They see the interrelationships among the parts and try to create synergies to ensure smooth functioning. They balance the often conflicting needs of their employees, shareholders, and customers. They are holistic in their approaches. They know that tampering with one part of the system will have an impact on other parts. They realize that their organizations don't operate in cocoons. They see how their organizations influence the marketplace and how the marketplace buffers them. And they are proactive in ensuring that their organizations not only survive, but thrive.

This section will have greater application for people at the top of their organizations. However, those leaders who are aiming to the higher echelons of their organizations will find it useful too, as they will need to understand the thinking and strategies that occupy the thoughts of top management.

Alliances

He who has a thorough knowledge of his own condition as
well as the conditions of the enemy is sure to win in all battles.
He who has a thorough knowledge of his own conditions but not the
conditions of the enemy, has an even chance of winning or losing
the battle. He who has neither a thorough knowledge of his own
conditions nor of the enemy, is sure to lose in every battle.

—Sun-Tzu, *The Art of War*

Strategic alliances are not a new management fad. They are a response to a shrinking economy and circumstances that can change with bewildering speed. Alliances are excellent vehicles to enhance the growth and reach of an organization, enabling it to:

✓ enter new markets
✓ increase market share
✓ gain access to new techniques
✓ share risks
✓ access additional resources
✓ reduce costs by rationalizing activities

Alliances work particularly well when the parties:

✓ give clear and agreed-upon objectives
✓ are anxious to cooperate and achieve success

✓ provide adequate resources to ensure success
✓ organize and manage the enterprise effectively
✓ complement each other's skills
✓ have realistic expectations of the difficulties and opportunities

There are three major forms of alliances:

1. joint ventures
2. research and development (R&D) consortia
3. strategic alliances

JOINT VENTURES

✓ A joint venture is a business organization between companies, formed for the achievement of common goals.
✓ This form of business is often chosen as a vehicle for entering foreign markets where foreign ownership may be restricted.
✓ Joint ventures are generally defined by an equity ownership, with parties typically represented on the board in proportion to their ownership.
✓ Ownership splits typically reflect the size of each organization. A seventy-thirty split would result from one partner being much smaller than the other.

R&D CONSORTIA

✓ Sometimes the cost of developing a new product or process is incredibly difficult because:
  • the costs are too high for one organization to bear
  • the expertise is only available elsewhere
  • the development timelines are extremely long

✓ R&D consortia take advantage of the availability of sophisticated communication, planning, and design tools to enable virtual teams to work collaboratively from any part of the world.

✔ Before committing to an R&D partnership, ask yourself if you:
- Have protected your contribution.
- Understand the intellectual property laws of other countries you'll be operating in. Check with others who have ventured into those countries to learn what mistakes they might have made that you can avoid.

STRATEGIC ALLIANCES

Strategic alliances are relationships between two or more organizations that bring about synergies that they could not achieve individually. Usually each organization has strengths and abilities that the other is lacking. A typical example is a relationship in which one organization has developed a product and the other has a strong marketing and sales organization that has an established presence in the marketplace.

Deciding on whether an organization could benefit from some form of alliance is best done through a strategic-planning exercise. Such an exercise will include a SWOT analysis—strengths, weaknesses, opportunities, and threats.

Determining whether you have chosen the right partner is a function of a number of factors. Consider the following issues.

✔ Do you have complementary skills?
✔ Can you envision working effectively with the partner, bearing in mind any cultural differences?
✔ Has the potential partner had a history of successful relationships with other partners?
✔ Is the partner fully committed?
✔ Is the partner trustworthy?

The effort taken to find the right partner will pay handsomely, as it will help to avoid delays, misunderstandings, subpar performance, and the likelihood of a breakup.

Benchmarking

Bench*mark*ing *n*, a continuous, systematic process for evaluating the products, services, and work processes of organizations that are recognized as representing best practices for the purpose of organizational improvement.
—Michael J. Spendolini, *The Benchmarking Book*, 1992

As a leader, you have the onerous obligation of meeting the needs of all your stakeholders. And as you do, you will find that their expectations rise, so the process of meeting those needs is ongoing. Finding new and better ways of doing what you are doing is challenging. Ideas may come spontaneously from your employees or they can come from a deliberate effort to establish your organization as best in class. Benchmarking is the process of identifying, studying, and learning outstanding practices from outside sources to help your organization improve its performance.

✓ What is benchmarking?
- Benchmarking is the deliberate, systematic process whereby an organization seeks to find out who the best are, to learn from them, and to adapt and implement new ideas to improve customer satisfaction.
- Benchmarking typically focuses on business processes—all the steps it takes to provide a service or product to a client.
- Organizations have hundreds of processes, all of which have some degree of imperfection. Our processes are inconsistent—sometimes they are right, sometimes wrong; sometimes fast, sometimes slow.

Benchmarking helps us identify strategies to improve our processes dramatically.

✓ Why benchmark?
- Benchmarking attempts to provide an organization with a yardstick, or standard, by which to judge itself. It is hard to envision how much better you could be until you check out the possibilities by establishing who the champions are, and how good they are.
- To avoid benchmarking can be the kiss of death for an organization, since its leaders may have false illusions about their effectiveness. They may become defensive at the thought of discovering they are less than perfect.

✓ What can I benchmark?
- Although early benchmarking was focused primarily on manufacturing, it is now common practice to compare any process against the best in class.
- Deciding which processes to benchmark should be prioritized according to:
  - how much they affect the bottom line (that is, have the highest potential for cost reduction)
  - the number of customer complaints they generate
  - how easily they can be fixed
  - whether there are many similar processes in other organizations

✓ Where can I get the information?
- Avoid the mistake of looking for best practices in your own backyard. The farther afield you go, the more likely you are to find interesting, innovative ideas. Many industries besides your own have similar processes—hiring, selling, design, delivery, to name a few—that may be carried out quite differently, offering you an opportunity to learn about and implement significantly improved methods.
- The world is your oyster. Look inside your own industry for informa-

tion on specialized processes, but beyond your industry for generic processes.

✓ How do I collect the information? A variety of strategies can be used to gain information:

- *Industry Standards*. Many industry associations collect data from members and provide access to this data.
- *Cooperative Benchmarking*. In this process, a number of organizations agree to pool their knowledge and share it among themselves.
- *Competitive Benchmarking*. This process enables an organization to study the practices of the competition without their cooperation. Information can be obtained by using the product or service and studying it from the inside. The process of buying a product and dismantling it to find out its characteristics is known as reverse engineering.

✓ How is the benchmarking process carried out?

- Plan the process. Decide which approach works best.
- Pick a process or a group of related processes to benchmark.
- Form a team that will oversee the process.
- Invite potential partners to join the information-sharing group. Meet with them and have them sign a confidentiality agreement, especially if they have associated businesses in a related field. Agree on the areas of information sharing and the process whereby this will take place.
- Decide how you will measure the resulting change in performance. Typical indicators would measure improved quality, speed, or cost reduction. Establish current measures before the benchmarking takes place so that benefits can be tracked.
- Prepare for the study. Create a list of questions that need to be covered.
- Study the processes in question. Confirm understandings to make sure the team agrees on what it has learned.

- Analyze the data. Have the team members review their findings together. They should document:
  - what they have learned
  - what actions they recommend
  - the benefits of those actions
- Implement as many of the recommendations as possible. This will demonstrate respect for the team and the research, as well as a commitment to foster innovative practices.
- Track to ensure that benefits are achieved. Monitor the measures. If goals are achieved, reward those responsible appropriately. If targets are not achieved, find out why before the next benchmarking exercise in order to ensure that it will be more successful.

Change:
Influencing the Future

Change is the law of life. And those who look only to the
past or present are certain to miss the future.

—John F. Kennedy

An important leadership task is to influence events or people. A leader needs to promote continuous innovation and performance improvement. On the other hand, people rarely welcome change. Most are comfortable with the status quo.

Driving change will be less challenging if you adopt these strategies:

- ✓ Take a prominent role. Be seen to be leading the change. Make yourself available to explain new initiatives. Be there to celebrate improvements.
- ✓ Challenge the people around you. Ask everyone to stretch. Set challenging goals with—not for—individuals and teams. Reward those who excel.
- ✓ Create a strong team. It's lonely at the top, so surround yourself with capable players who are aligned with your goals and values. Have them also act as ambassadors for change. Remove team members who are unable to grasp opportunities or lead those around them. Changing players sends a very strong signal about your determination to achieve success.

✓ Adjust your strategy to the level of urgency required. Sometimes ideas that are not urgent can be allowed to percolate slowly throughout the organization. These ideas can be incorporated into training programs that can be cascaded, step by step, through the organization. However, if an idea needs to be accepted quickly, the leadership role must change. Senior people need to associate themselves with the concept and be seen to champion the cause at every opportunity.

✓ Expand the team to incorporate change leaders. Sometimes momentum can be achieved by bringing on board additional leaders whose high energy, can-do attitude, and clear thinking can help you move the strategy forward.

✓ Embrace new ideas, even though some people see them as fads. Sure, "fad" has a pejorative connotation, and some will see the new idea as the flavor of month. But new programs can make a contribution, even though they may die later on. Make the most of a new concept by using these strategies:

  • Test its effectiveness in a pilot. Learn from the implementation. Fine-tune it to remove the bugs and try it in a second area. When you're sure that you've removed most of the bugs (you'll never remove them all) roll it out in other parts of the organization.

  • Fine-tune implementation and rollout so that success and credibility increase with time. This will also increase the perception that the program is homegrown.

  • Gain commitment from all levels of management before widespread rollout. Do so by:
    • Communicating the reasons for the initiative.
    • Avoiding the word "program." Refer to it as a process, since processes are ongoing.
    • Demonstrating top-management commitment.
    • Inviting suggestions as to how the initiative can become successful. Avoid discussions on roadblocks, because you are guaranteed to hear the same old recycled excuses of lack of time, lack of people, etc.

- Communicating "what's in it for them."
- Clarifying accountability.
- Using testimonials from successful programs.
- Stressing realistic expectations. Positioning the new process as the best thing since winning the lottery will merely serve to increase cynicism.
- Emphasizing that the new initiative is not meant as a cure-all. Rather, it will serve to improve effectiveness in one area, such as teamwork, service, measurement, effectiveness, or leadership.
- Before implementing a new idea, find out as much about it as possible. Downplay the claims about benefits and simplicity that are part of the package offered by the consultant. Treat the opinions of the sponsoring department with equal caution. Listen to peers in other organizations who can attest to the rewards as well as the challenges.

✓ Communicate—clearly, concisely, and consistently. Hold information meetings to ensure that the grapevine does not spread the wrong message.
- Plan what you intend to say. Think about starting off with a message that connects you with the audience. Then get into the details, showing that you have a plan and that you have considered their interests. Highlight the benefits. End with a message that inspires action and stresses commitment—yours and theirs.
- Think about your employees and frame your comments in the context of their perspectives. They will likely be received more openly.
- Use the language that employees are likely to use, bearing in mind their backgrounds, education, and positions in the organization.
- Simplify complex issues. Explain topics by giving examples wherever possible.
- Look bad news square in the face. Don't sweep difficult issues under the carpet. But do try and put a positive spin on the issue by showing

the good that will result from the change, while recognizing the challenges.

- Leave time for questions. If none are forthcoming, ask some of the more outspoken—but positive—people what issues they may have. Encourage others to join in by thanking each person for his or her questions, no matter how tough they may be.

31

Communicating with the Board and Other Executives

Words mean more than what is set down on paper. It takes the human voice to infuse them with the shades of deeper meaning.

—Maya

Whenever you have a great idea, you have to sell it upward as well as downward. This means getting buy-in not only from your team and your peers but also from your bosses—top management or even the board. By following a few key principles you can make the higher-ups as keen on your ideas as you are.

✓ Understand that selling new ideas is a key part of leadership. So, be ready to articulate new ideas and directions to other colleagues with whom you share power.

✓ Prepare, prepare, prepare.
  • Accumulate as much backup information as you can find. The more novel or controversial your idea, the more supporting documentation you will need.
  • Rehearse your presentation beforehand with a colleague, a friend in the same field, or your mentor. Remember to put together a written package to support your presentation, and have your "test audience" review that as well.
  • Tap into the hot topics of the day. Know beforehand what's on the agenda of your audience so that you can align your needs with

theirs. For example, if senior management's focus is on cost cutting, emphasize how your idea will save money.

- Research the values and beliefs of your audience so that your pitch will be in sync with those attitudes.
- Make sure your promises and predictions or claims are realistic. Senior management can usually smell snake oil from a mile off.
- Try out revolutionary ideas on a skeptic, not your friends. Friends are likely to tell you what you want to hear rather than the truth. Allow the skeptic to tear your idea apart, giving you the opportunity to prepare answers to the most difficult questions.

✓ Present like a pro.
- Greet the executive(s) warmly. Shake hands firmly and hold the handshake a second longer than usual. Smile with your whole face.
- Project optimism. Be an evangelist. But don't try to hide a bad idea behind hyperbole. Ideas delivered with enthusiasm get more buy-in than those wrapped in a cloud of gloom.
- Focus on benefits instead of features. Senior people are not interested in how things work—that's the function of the operating employees. What they want to know is the likely revenue or savings impact of the new product or service on time, money, or other resources.
- Speak the language of the audience that you are pitching. What kind of people are they? Are they analytical? If so, be prepared with the numbers. If they are more likely to be driven by emotion, be ready to supplement your presentation with anecdotes about people and motivation.
- Be brief and to the point. Senior managers operate under severe time constraints, and their attention spans can be quite limited. If you have a lot of supporting documentation, make up a handout to go with your presentation.
- Check for understanding from time to time without embarrassing the audience. Glazed eyes, lack of eye contact, and looking at watches are clues that you've lost their attention. To regain your

audience, change the pace briefly by modulating your voice or asking for an opinion.

- Help others to see your ideas. Build a picture in their minds or show them what you are after. The better your listeners understand, the more likely they are to buy in. Remember, a picture is worth a thousand words.
- Make sure that you do not run over your allotted time, and provide adequate opportunities for questions.
- Keep your eyes on the audience at all times. Do not look at notes or the screen—you will seem to be displaying lack of conviction. Worse still, you won't be able to see subtle changes in body language that will give you clues about your audience's level of enthusiasm.
- Avoid too much detail. Typically the listeners will be big-picture people who are interested in your conclusions (that is, the benefits) rather than the details of your research. Should anyone need further detail, the numbers can be provided in useful handouts.
- Choose your words carefully. The right words can captivate and the wrong words can spell disaster. Avoid exaggeration and words such as "always" and "never," or adjectives that connote lack of factual evidence, such as "amazing," "fabulous," or "exceptional." You could be challenged to show the evidence behind your hyperbole, and that could damage the credibility of your entire presentation.
- Make sure that you are being understood. Listen to and show interest in the reactions of your audience, and respond to them. This will demonstrate the importance you place on their opinions.
- Engage the audience—without getting sidetracked—whenever possible.
- Give compliments if they are appropriate and where they are due. Genuine compliments, especially those on topic with your idea, will warm your audience to you and encourage further interaction.
- If you don't get immediate buy-in, determine the objections and request a follow-up meeting at which you can address them. And don't whine.

✓ Follow up quickly.

- In a memo, thank the people who attended your presentation as soon as possible. This memo should address the main issues raised by the audience and indicate your determination to deal with them immediately.

- Gather information about outstanding objections (if there are any) and implementation (if you got immediate approval) and put this information in a report to senior management. Don't let the idea rest until a decision is made.

Consultants: Getting Your Money's Worth

Needing someone is like needing a parachute. If they are not there the first time you need them, the chances are you won't be needing them again.

—Scott Adams

For one reason or another, most consulting assignments start with great excitement and hoopla. But few fulfill their promises. And, despite your best efforts, there may be occasions when you feel that your money was not well spent and time was wasted. You will know you have made a poor investment if:

✓ the majority of trainees considered the training a waste of time
✓ you paid a premium price for a poor product
✓ the consultant's conduct was unprofessional and resulted in complaints
✓ promised workbooks and videos for the session were not provided

Here are some follow-up techniques that can minimize the impact of costly consulting mistakes:

✓ Negotiate for a reduced fee for the work already done.
✓ Negotiate for reduced fees for upcoming initiatives.
✓ Ask the consultant to prepare a recovery strategy at no extra cost.

✓ Ask the consultant to provide some value-added service, such as training, at little or no cost.

✓ As a mutual learning opportunity, discuss the outcome with the consultant.

✓ Apologize to employees for any mistakes made by the consultant. Make it clear that that is not the company way!

✓ If you generally like the services of the consulting firm but are disappointed with one specific representative, ask for a replacement for the rest of the project.

✓ Conduct follow-up research to ensure that you are not reacting to opinions expressed by only a few malcontents.

✓ If initial reviews are poor for long-term projects, pay a penalty fee to discontinue the initiative rather than hoping for the best.

✓ Use every poor consulting experience as an opportunity to understand your role in setting realistic expectations.

Consultants have rights too. It is difficult for them to provide appropriate service when companies don't deliver promised information or access to background material. Changing delivery dates, canceling meetings, or delaying payments is unprofessional—and behavior that you would never tolerate in a consultant.

Consultants: Maximizing Value for Your Organization

A consultant is a person who uses your watch to tell you what time it is.

—Grey Owl (Archibald Belaney)

For every consulting success story there's one about poor service, outrageous prices, and dashed expectations. The increased availability of consulting firms and independent training entrepreneurs presents greater choices than ever before. Checking credibility can be a challenge, but no organization can afford poor service.

✓ Consultants provide a number of advantages:
- up-to-date training expertise in specialized areas
- lower-cost solutions for repeated training needs or one-time-only initiatives
- a fresh perspective for employees
- labor market information gained from working with a number of companies or industries
- responsiveness in meeting tight deadlines
- skills and programs that are not available in-house

✓ Some disadvantages in dealing with consultants are that they:
- are less committed to your organization's long-term success
- cost more, on an hourly basis, than internally trained employees

- work for your competitors too, and may jeopardize confidentiality
- may not have an in-depth appreciation of your organization's culture
- will want to be paid no matter how successful (or unsuccessful) the initiative is

✓ Managers are bombarded with calls from consultants offering their services. Here are some suggestions for managing a high volume of unsolicited calls:
- *Never* be rude. You represent your organization at all times, and any bad manners on your part reflects on your company.
- Request literature from consultants before agreeing to a meeting. This material will give you both a sense of the professionalism of the consultant and some client references.
- Designate one afternoon a month to meet with prospective consultants. If nothing else, you can pick their brains for new ideas.
- Prepare a semiannual summary of your training needs to send to callers so that you hear back only from those who are able to meet your requirements.
- Ask callers about their industry expertise, client references, and credentials in the area that they are pitching.
- Ask callers about their perspectives on training trends and organizational challenges to gain a sense of their experience.
- Keep all the literature you receive from consultants during the year. It's an excellent source of competitive information and research.

✓ Before hiring a consultant, find out the following:
- How good is the consultant's reputation? You don't judge a book by its cover, so don't base your evaluation on the slickness of the consultant's brochures or the performance of a presentation.
- How did the consultant contact you? Was it a through a reference or a cold call?
- What makes the consultant uniquely qualified to help you with the particular challenges you have?

- How credible are the consultant's references?
- How similar have the consultant's other assignments been to your own, and how effective was the training?

✓ During an interview meeting with a consultant, establish:
- What makes the consultant's organization special. What innovative work has the consultant done?
- Whether the consultant is using your organization as a test site for a new program.
- How flexible the consultant is about your specific issues, for example, costs, size of the pilot program (if any), time requirements of your employees, etc.
- Whether the consultant will provide a written outline of the program, including course objectives.
- How the effectiveness of the intervention will be measured.
- If any guarantees of improvement are given in measurable formats.
- The professional qualifications and experience of the consultant who will be working on your assignment.
- Whether the person selling the assignment will be responsible for implementation too.
- The personality and background of the consultant. Given the culture of your organization, will that style fit?
- How flexible the program will be in terms of meeting your time horizons and deadlines.
- Whether your employees will have a hotline to the trainer whenever they need support or advice.
- What homework the consultant has done about your organization's size, market niche, competitive edge, and product lines.
- How competitive the fee structure is compared to others in the field.
- Whether the quoted prices are all-inclusive or if there are additional costs (for duplication of materials, travel, etc.).
- Whether and how often the consultant has published articles in

respected journals or newspapers or spoken at high-profile conferences.

- Whether the consultant does any government work (governments are very strict about qualifying consultants).
- If the trainer has backup for a scheduled course in case of sickness or other emergency.
- If the consultant belongs to any recognized professional associations.
- How long the consultant or consulting organization has been in business.
- If the consultant has relevant experience in your industry.

Governance: More Than Staying Out of Jail

Even in a time of elephantine vanity and greed, one never has
to look far to see the campfires of gentle people.

—Garrison Keillor

In the light of an alarming number of high-profile cases of theft, greed, and misuse of corporate assets, directors and senior corporate leaders have been pushed into drastically changing the way organizational assets are taken care of. This process is known as governance.

Governance is about the influence of stakeholders in the affairs and direction of an organization. It reflects their interests, how their views are included in decisions, how decisions are made, and how the decision makers are held accountable.

Governance is not about restrictions. It is more about creating democratic processes in organizations to enable and encourage freedom of initiative and enterprise. This freedom is designed to build trust among all the stakeholders so that they can focus on their goals, create world-class products and services, and optimize financial benefits for shareholders and employees.

Improving governance requires that we strengthen and change the relationship that the board has with the corporation. It requires that the board uses increased power to ensure compliance of the officers of the organization to all standards set by government and other outside regulatory bodies.

Legislation alone will not lead to significant improvements in governance. The attitude of senior management is key.

✓ Good governance is the responsibility of all executives as well as the board. Good governance will enhance the performance of an organization if the executive team:
  - takes a longer-term focus on financial performance, beyond quarterly results
  - supports a strong board that is independent of those running the daily affairs of the organization
  - establishes methods for listening to the shareholders and responding to their needs
  - ensures that it does not become ensnarled in defensive activities that detract from management's ability to take risks
  - promotes strategic planning and the execution of those plans
  - emphasizes and promotes success instead of avoiding failure

✓ At the heart of good governance is accountability. The benefits of increased accountability include:
  - Increased employee confidence in the organization.
  - More effective use of assets.
  - Greater debate within an organization as to how better to allocate resources to competing priorities. The creativity that flows from this debate will lead to improved performance.
  - Increased participation by investors willing to contribute knowledge capital, as well as financial capital, in order to boost shareholder value.

✓ Good governance is characterized by these factors:
  - *Involvement*. All members are capable of being heard.
  - *Transparency*. Information is available to all.
  - *Consensus Decisions*. Attempts are made, when practical, to achieve broad agreement to decisions.

- *Equity*. All people, no matter what race, age, color, creed, gender, or sexual orientation, have an equal ability to participate.
- *Effectiveness*. The organization's resources are utilized effectively.
- *Accountability*. Decision makers are responsible for their behavior.
- *Strategic Vision*. There is agreement about the general direction and influence of the organization.

✓ Good governance requires that the board and the CEO become independent of one another so as to prevent collusion. Ideally:
- The chairperson and CEO roles should be occupied by different people.
- The CEO should be nonvoting.
- In strategy formulation and policymaking, the CEO will be seen as a full partner with the board.
- The board will focus on monitoring performance rather than formulating policies.
- The CEO will attend all board meetings and participate fully in all discussions.
- In large organizations, the board will monitor performance through standing committees, including an audit body.

✓ The board does not involve itself in the day-to-day running of the organization—that is the task of the CEO and his or her management team. The primary tasks of the board are to:
- create a strategic plan, which sets the course for the organization
- regularly update the strategic plan as circumstances change
- set the organization's direction, ensuring that it has a compelling mission
- develop clear objectives stemming from the mission
- create a set of values to ensure that the corporation operates effectively and professionally
- ensure that the assets of the corporation are being effectively utilized

✓ Good governance often means change. Here are some specific actions that may demonstrate your organization's good intentions.

- Increasing the number of independent directors to the point where they form a majority on the board. Size matters, depending on the nature of the organization and the complexity of its operations. As a general guide, however, the board should be made up of between five and seven members.
- Ensuring that all committee members are nonmanagement in order to ensure that decision making is impartial.
- Conducting some board meetings without management present, ensuring open and candid discussions.
- Promoting stock ownership (in the case of for-profit companies) so that directors have a stake in the long-term success of the organization.
- Seeking shareholder approval for significant change in systems of compensation for senior executives.
- Promoting the concept of pay-for-performance rather than stock options. Rather, bonuses and "performance share units" should be linked to specific performance objectives—cash flow, profits, or customer satisfaction—rather than stock price.
- Seeking third-party professional advice when reviewing and evaluating compensation practices.
- Separating the role of chairperson of the board from those of president and CEO. The chairperson should be seen as the chief governance officer.
- Separating the audit and risk-management committees to recognize the importance and contribution of each. These committees should be viewed as committees of the board, not autonomous entities.
- Designing compensation plans for executives who are aligned with corporate strategy rather than with short-term share value increases.
- Enhancing the competence of directors by creating position descriptions for the chairs of each committee and the chairperson of the board. Then—scary as this may be—have each director assess him-

self and each other. When shortcomings are identified, have each person develop a plan for improvement. Any director refusing to improve should be removed.

Here is a checklist to help senior leaders assess their effectiveness in the area of governance:

GOVERNANCE: AN EFFECTIVE EVALUATION FOR BOARDS OF DIRECTORS

1. Board members are given orientation to prepare them for fulfilling their governance responsibilities.

   Strongly Agree   Agree   Neither Agree nor Disagree   Disagree   Strongly Disagree

2. The board is actively involved in planning the direction and priorities of the organization.

   Strongly Agree   Agree   Neither Agree nor Disagree   Disagree   Strongly Disagree

3. The board evaluates the performance of the CEO against measurable performance objectives.

   Strongly Agree   Agree   Neither Agree nor Disagree   Disagree   Strongly Disagree

4. The board understands and clearly defines its role and that of the CEO.

   Strongly Agree   Agree   Neither Agree nor Disagree   Disagree   Strongly Disagree

5. The CEO is solely accountable to the board, as everything is delegated through him/her.

   Strongly Agree   Agree   Neither Agree nor Disagree   Disagree   Strongly Disagree

6. The board has representatives of all the key stakeholders, including shareholders, customers, and employees.

   Strongly Agree   Agree   Neither Agree nor Disagree   Disagree   Strongly Disagree

7. Board members formulate and adopt the organization's mission and values.

Strongly Agree   Agree   Neither Agree nor Disagree   Disagree   Strongly Disagree

8. The board demonstrates commitment to the organization's mission and values.

Strongly Agree   Agree   Neither Agree nor Disagree   Disagree   Strongly Disagree

9. Board members comply with the requirements outlined in key elements of the governance structure (for example, bylaws, policies, code of conduct).

Strongly Agree   Agree   Neither Agree nor Disagree   Disagree   Strongly Disagree

10. The board and the CEO have a productive working relationship.

Strongly Agree   Agree   Neither Agree nor Disagree   Disagree   Strongly Disagree

11. The board is capable of handling any major strategic crisis that can reasonably be anticipated.

Strongly Agree   Agree   Neither Agree nor Disagree   Disagree   Strongly Disagree

12. Board meetings are effective. (The agenda is drawn up by the chairperson with input from the CEO. Meetings are evaluated to ensure that objectives have been achieved.)

Strongly Agree   Agree   Neither Agree nor Disagree   Disagree   Strongly Disagree

13. The board uses sound decision-making processes that focus on board responsibilities, reliable factual information, etc.

Strongly Agree   Agree   Neither Agree nor Disagree   Disagree   Strongly Disagree

14. The organization exhibits a good balance between stability and innovation.

Strongly Agree   Agree   Neither Agree nor Disagree   Disagree   Strongly Disagree

15. The board meets periodically without senior management. From time to time the CEO invites senior managers to provide the board with additional, in-depth information on a subject of interest.

Strongly Agree   Agree   Neither Agree nor Disagree   Disagree   Strongly Disagree

16. Board recruitment reflects a diversity of interests and personalities.

Strongly Agree   Agree   Neither Agree nor Disagree   Disagree   Strongly Disagree

17. The board chairperson is a strong leader who is an expert in corporate governance practices.

Strongly Agree   Agree   Neither Agree nor Disagree   Disagree   Strongly Disagree

18. The board is encouraged to challenge conventional wisdom and existing practices without personalizing differences.

Strongly Agree   Agree   Neither Agree nor Disagree   Disagree   Strongly Disagree

19. The board is recruited from people who have no allegiance to top management.

Strongly Agree   Agree   Neither Agree nor Disagree   Disagree   Strongly Disagree

20. Board members are encouraged to ask questions, particularly as they relate to aspects of the organization in which they have limited expertise.

Strongly Agree   Agree   Neither Agree nor Disagree   Disagree   Strongly Disagree

Governance: Structuring the Board of Directors

Competence, like truth, beauty and contact lenses, is in the eye of the beholder.
—Laurence J. Peter, *The Peter Principle* (1969)

Government legislation to purge organizations of conflicts of interest, false accounting, and shareholder abuse seems to be beginning to work, as the headlines revealing massive frauds appear to be subsiding quickly. But organizations that are run by boards dominated by friends and family of the CEO are still under increased fire. How can a board with close personal ties to the CEO be truly objective and look after the needs of the shareholders above all?

Board practices need to change. Here's how to endear the board to the shareholders and the financial community:

✓ Choose board members who have:
- high profiles in the community
- ability to open important doors, particularly those of major customers or government
- diversity of expertise
- diversity of gender and ethnicity
- industry knowledge

✓ Recruit the majority of board members from outside the organization. The higher the percentage of outside board members, the greater will be the objectivity and usefulness of the board. This is an especially difficult challenge for family-owned and entrepreneurial organizations.

✓ Effective boards are deliberately created. Members are given training and a comprehensive orientation as part of their initiations. They should:

- familiarize themselves with the nature of the business
- meet with senior managers individually in order to understand key issues (at the same time, they must ensure that they avoid interfering in day-to-day operations)
- be given a detailed understanding of the organization's accounting practices
- appoint fully independent audit, nominating, and compensation committees
- meet periodically *without* senior management to discuss the performance of managers, the board, and committees
- draft charters for board committees
- adopt corporate governance guidelines
- create a code of conduct and ethics for the board (including rules for conflicts of interest) and directors' qualification standards

✓ Some people argue that the CEO should be a member of the board but NOT be a voting member. In such a case, however, the CEO will still:

- be influential in policy making
- participate in all meetings and discussions
- be a full partner in all matters short of voting (that is, decision making) and carry out the day-to-day operations of the organization within the guidelines set by the board

✓ In terms of the distribution of power and areas of accountability, there is a difference between a results-oriented board and a traditional board. A results-oriented board will focus on the larger picture and ensure that day-to-day operations are being carried out within the scope and guidelines set by the board. To achieve the organization's goals, the board should have four subcommittees:

- *Executive Committee*. This committee deals with matters of urgency between board meetings. Members have specific powers and limitations established by the board.
- *Governance Committee*. This committee ensures that governance practices are being implemented or improved. As such it must be objective and not include any senior managers or anyone related to the CEO. This committee develops governance processes and conducts regular audits to ensure that they are operating effectively.
- *Audit (Quality Assurance) Committee*. The board of directors needs to monitor business practices separately from the auditors who work closely with the operating executives. The mandate of this committee is to assess risk. To do this, the committee should independently monitor the organization's financial reporting process and internal control systems. It also coordinates reviews and appraises the audit process of the outside accountants. Typically a group of three outside board members identifies the eight to twelve major risks facing the organization. They evaluate the probability of these contingencies occurring and the extent to which the organization is prepared to meet them.
- *Compensation Committee*. This independent committee has the challenging task of establishing compensation for the senior executives. Its task is to ensure that the compensation packages are:
  - reasonable
  - competitive
  - in line with the efforts and successes of the executives
  - related to performance goals that benefit all stakeholders

These committees report to the board and provide it with recommendations for approval. The committees are there to do the legwork in their areas of specialization, but are subject to the mandate and decision-making authority of the board.

✓ A manual of policies and procedures should be established to ensure that everyone is aware of:

- the mandate of standing governance committees
- who is accountable for what
- how meetings are to be run, including roles, frequencies, and deliverables
- the nature and frequency of reports due from the different committees

Government:
Managing Relationships

The thing I enjoyed most were visits from children.
They did not want public office.

—Herbert Hoover

As a senior member of your organization you will come into contact with legislators, government officials, and regulatory bodies. These folks are different. Some of them are there at the behest of a politician. Others are long-term employees who have a vested interest in the status quo. But all of them want to look good, and most want to serve as (or be seen to be) custodians of the public interest. Those who survive the system usually have great political savvy. They need to be dealt with deliberately and with care because they can negatively influence your organization—and your career. Here are the tools and techniques to ensure a smooth and productive relationship.

✓ *Always do your homework.* Be prepared. Know whom you are dealing with. Find out who the movers and shakers are in the ministry/ department/office you are seeking to influence. Make these people your allies. Get to know them. Find out their hot buttons. See how you can position your needs so that they appear to match the objectives of the policy makers. Align yourself with key decision makers without upsetting the people in the back rooms. In fact, find out who the backroom people are and which ones have their bosses' attention.

✓ *Keep up to date.* Be aware of the evolving climate of opinion within government, the media, and relevant interest groups. Know what they are saying about issues that affect you. Read as much as you can about current issues in your industry. And keep your finger on the pulse of legislation that may have a bearing on your organization.

✓ *Get to know the key decision makers.* Learn to understand them. Find out what works best from others who have influenced them. Don't adopt an in-your-face approach if a subtle one would work best.

✓ *Know the hot buttons of the day.* Wherever possible, express your thoughts and needs within the framework the decision makers use. Know the issues on their radar screens and ensure that they are on yours too!

✓ *Anticipate roadblocks.* Consider how you will deal with them. Be prepared for the unexpected.

✓ *Network continuously.* Keep open the channels of communication with your key target people. Make them feel that you consider them friends and allies. Maintain ongoing contact and information exchange. This will build up credits so that you can sometimes ask for help too. The balance of favors provided must appear to tip toward the person who can help you, and not vice versa.

✓ *Treat others as you want to be treated.* Deal with each person as special and unique. Avoid making enemies. Don't always say what you think—it may not go down well, even if it is the truth. Always interact with courtesy and empathy. Respect people whether they are helping or hindering you. You never know when they will have a change of heart—for better or for worse.

✓ *Behave in a constructive manner.* Avoid conflict. Make the issues of others your issues. Avoid taking extreme positions. Be seen to be reasonable, if not in your ideas, at least in how they are presented. Strive for win-win situations.

✓ *Be patient.* Timing is everything. Wait for the right moment to make your move. Determine when the momentum is swinging your way because public sentiment is at a high point, the news media are on board, or committees are being established to make recommendations in areas of interest. And remember, be prepared to intervene early on issues in order to influence emerging demands, changing priorities, and new policies—long before problems arise.

✓ *Don't waste people's time.* Respect their need to deal with issues quickly. If you need more time, meet with them outside of their environments whenever possible, as they are bound to be more relaxed outside the office.

✓ *Present your case with confidence.* Use all the power you can muster. The more power you have, the more influential you will be. Your power will come from the following:

- *Legitimacy*. Present your issues convincingly, in a professional, balanced, and accurate way, and always backed by solid documentation, preferably by recognized experts.

- *Rationality*. Always highlight the facts before expressing an opinion. In fact, hold back your opinions where the facts you present are irrefutable.

- *Precedent*. Show examples of success from other jurisdictions where circumstances are similar.

- *Numbers*. Form coalitions so that potential naysayers will see they are up against a groundswell of people and/or organizations. Use petitions, letters, faxes, and e-mails from as many people as possible to ensure that the decision makers understand you are part of a large majority.

✓ *Participate enthusiastically.* Be active on committees and task forces that will make decisions and recommendations that will affect you. Make sure that you get into the back rooms as well as the front office. Join committees that influence the decision makers. Be a part of the process, not a witness from the sidelines. Make sure that you are assertive in advocating for your constituency, that you stay "on message," and that your position is always known.

Integration: Creating a United Organization

Who looks outside, dreams; Who looks inside, awakens.

—Carl Jung

Historians suggest that the modern organization is based on a model established by the Ming dynasty in China some six hundred years ago to maintain a large, far-flung empire. It was based on three principles: divide and conquer, command, and control. Improving your lot in life depended on your ability to please your supervisors. In the belief that there was no alternative, this model was emulated by Western organizations for centuries. But the model has long since outlived its usefulness. It creates a bureaucratic organization that focuses inward and fights change tooth and nail. The model encourages competition among its component parts. It also encourages those at the top to see those at the bottom as incompetent and uncommitted, needing to be controlled by rules, policies, and discipline.

Although organizations have begun to change to meet the challenges of a rapidly evolving global economy, many have not, and they have paid a heavy price by going out of business. Creating fast, flexible, and outward-focused organizations is imperative for survival. These leadership activities will promote a more effective, integrated organization:

✓ *Create a vision.* A vision that stresses seamless processes, collaboration, and harmony promotes a supportive environment in which all the parts work together and share resources and information.

✓ *Live the vision.* Constantly emphasize the dangers of unhealthy competition and rivalry among divisions. Nevertheless, reward the areas that perform best, and especially those that assist others to perform better.

✓ *Dismantle fiefdoms.* Remove managers from departments and divisions that operate like islands, with little interest in the rest of the organization.

✓ *Study work processes and build departments around key processes.* It is not often that a client—whether internal or external—can be served from one work area. Processes bounce back and forth among work areas. This movement of activities among departments, known as handoffs, often results in delays and mistakes. Reducing the number of handoffs may require that work be reengineered so that people who are serving the same customers are colocated, helping to ensure that the process flow among them is seamless.

✓ *Set up reward systems that encourage collaboration.* Reward managers for openness, sharing, and collaboration. Celebrate acts of generosity among managers.

✓ *Create forums to exchange best practices.* Set up regular intracompany fairs where different parts of the organization can show off their best practices and feel the pride that comes from such innovations. This will allow all those attending to learn from each other and multiply those innovations many times across the organization.

✓ *Exchange employees.* Encourage employees to work in different parts of the organization in order to give them exposure to its other aspects. This is especially valuable if your organization has operations around the world. Learning new cultures and new approaches to doing business will build a generation of leaders who are global in their thinking and empathetic in dealing with other parts of the organization.

✓ *Set up cross-functional teams.* Difficult problems require creativity and commitment from as many sources as possible. In order to get the maximum buy-in for change, create focused problem-solving teams comprising representatives from areas that have traditionally been antagonistic.

International Operations

Start by doing what's necessary; then do what's possible;
and suddenly you are doing the impossible.

—St. Francis of Assisi

Events of the last quarter-century have dramatically changed the way business is done, especially for medium and larger companies that can now do business in countries that were previously behind the Iron Curtain. The opening of borders has created incredible opportunities to access faster-growing markets and to identify new sources of lower-cost production. Strategic partnerships, alliances, and branch plants are increasingly commonplace. Faster transportation and instant communications allow people to work around the globe as part of a team as if they were at the same location. The new executive has a global perspective, speaks multiple languages, and understands different cultures.

Here are some tips to be able to thrive in the global market:

✓ Use technology to your advantage. Identify all your resources—Internet, intranet, satellite TV, global positioning systems, cell phones—and adopt them together with your business partners.

✓ Become superflexible. Not only do you need to adjust to each new culture you're dealing with, but you also need to keep abreast of the sociopolitical changes that are happening daily in different parts of the world. Avoid a tendency to make comparisons with the way things are done "back home," which is often interpreted as demeaning the locals. Instead, look for the good in what you have to work with and let your hosts know how much you appreciate their unique approaches or contributions.

✓ If you hit a roadblock or things go sour on you, avoid blaming the local people or culture. Adopt a collaborative approach to fixing the problem. Creating victims only reduces your ability to work effectively with the local folks on an ongoing basis.

✓ Recruit people who are able to think and work globally. These people typically:
  • are well educated
  • were born abroad
  • have worked internationally
  • have family members who are supportive about frequent business trips
  • enjoy travel and adventure
  • are flexible and adaptable
  • are friendly and outgoing

✓ Examine and streamline your business processes. Ask yourself:
  • Are they geared to operating internationally?
  • Do our call centers offer help in multiple languages?
  • Is our Web site available in the major languages?
  • Can people access different customized services and processes?
  • Do we foster collaboration among international locations or are we territorial?

✓ Be a role model. Demonstrate to those around you the correct way to conduct business.

✓ Make yourself comfortable wherever you are. If you travel frequently to the same place, increase your comfort with local conditions by:
  • Using the same taxi driver.
  • Staying at the same hotel. Decide on your favorite accommodation (location, floor, view, bed size) and have it prebooked. Leave some

clothing and toiletries at the hotel and have employees prepare the room for you before you arrive—it will give you a sense of "coming home."

- Frequenting the restaurants where you know the food is compatible with your constitution. Get to know the owner and waiters so that you are recognized when you return.

✓ Mold yourself into an international operator. Find local mentors in each part of the world in which you operate. Use their advice to ensure that your approach is consistent with local customs. Local agents are often ideal contacts, as they have an interest in collaborative relationships.

✓ Develop an anthropological mindset. See yourself as a researcher into new cultures. On each trip, make it your business to learn something new about the people you are working with. With time you will penetrate the surface of a new culture beyond the obvious (for example, food). Spend as much time as possible asking questions about people's attitudes, beliefs, family systems, decision making, relationships, conflict resolution strategies, fun activities, and history. Listen carefully and show your appreciation for the information provided. Avoid seeming judgmental in either words or body language.

✓ Avoid being boastful when people ask you about your culture, life, or work environment. Describe it in a matter-of-fact way without suggesting that it is any better.

✓ Communicate in the language of your host. Learn how people in your new environment interact. For example:
- Do they prefer one-on-one interaction, e-mail, or the phone?
- Do they expect you to listen more than you talk?
- Do they value getting to know you at a social level before they deal with you on a business level?
- Do they like to strike deals on the golf course, in the boardroom, at a coffee shop, or somewhere else?

- Do they expect to entertain you (that is, pick up the bill) or have you do so for them?
- Do they nod to acknowledge you or to indicate understanding?
- Do you check for understanding based on their verbal feedback or body language? Observe body language closely to identify the culture's signs of understanding, agreement, annoyance, or boredom.
- Do you avoid discussing topics that may be controversial? Get to know your new associates better before discussing politics, religion, or sex.

✓ When presenting in front of a foreign audience, be mindful of the barriers you face. Increase your probability of being understood and making an impact by:
- knowing your audience and their needs
- providing an introduction describing what you intend to cover and why it is important
- working slowly through the material, ensuring wherever possible that the audience is on board (because they say so or an interpreter assures you that it is so)
- using graphs and pictures to illustrate as many of the key points as possible
- stopping frequently to allow for questions

✓ Avoid stereotyping. Don't attribute certain characteristics—especially negative ones—to entire groups of people. You never know whose toes you may be stepping on.
✓ Operate ethically. Understand and clarify your own organization's standards in dealing with others, especially as it may relate to decisions such as:
- payments to foreign officials
- changes in labor practices
- real or perceived employee discrimination
- copyright infringements

✓ Working internationally requires, as always, that you get things done. Teamwork is key. Working in a virtual team is challenging enough, but doing so from different parts of the world is even more challenging. So enhance the effectiveness of your team by:

- Meeting together in person as often as is reasonable and practical.
- Using technology to its maximum advantage. The ability to communicate over the Internet using an inexpensive webcam allows for significant improvements in communications, as it enables people to see the expression on the other person's face. Cell phones can now be used to transfer images, and portable communication devices promote instant messaging. In addition, you should not hesitate to use the phone to clarify misperceptions that might be caused by different interpretations of the written word.

Partnerships

Destiny is not a matter of chance it is a matter of choice;
it is not a thing to be waited for, it is a thing to be achieved.
—William Jennings Bryan

Developing relationships with outside organizations is strategically important. So deciding whom to partner with and how to structure the relationship is also very important. There are a number of types of partnerships, varying from a loose coalition to serious integration on many levels. Here are some options for these relationships:

✓ *Collaborative Approach*. This approach is an agreement by two or more organizations to work together for their common good. Each organization is capable of providing a product or service to the other that can be made or done better by working closely together.

✓ *Financing/Sponsorship*. One organization in the process may be capable of adding value to the other but is challenged because of a lack of resources. The more resourceful company may make an investment or provide a loan to assist the undercapitalized organization.

✓ *Preferred Supplier/Vertical Integration*. In return for exceptional service and/or better prices, one organization may become the exclusive supplier of key products or services to another. The contract for such a relationship is longer term.

✓ *Strategic Alliance*. A strategic alliance is forged when significant synergies result from close cooperation between two equally strong organizations that have complementary strengths.

✓ *Joint Venture or Consortium.* Two or more organizations capitalize a new venture that draws on the resources and expertise of the founding partners.

✓ *Merger or Acquisition.* A merger is seen as the joining of two roughly equal partners to create an organization that is stronger than they are individually. Typically, some rationalization of their operations can be expected. With an acquisition, a larger, more powerful organization takes control of another to manage as it sees fit.

An increasing number of organizations are choosing to establish partnerships in order to strengthen their positions in the marketplace. The many and varied reasons for doing so include the following.

✓ *Strategic Reasons.* The organization may need to:
- respond quickly to changes in the industry
- expand, but be unable to provide the resources
- improve its corporate image
- align operations more closely to its vision and mission

✓ *Competitive Reasons.* The organization has found that:
- competitors are gaining market share at its expense
- competitors have formed effective strategic alliances
- it is struggling to differentiate itself in the marketplace
- the marketplace has become saturated

✓ *Marketing Reasons.* Management has realized that:
- there is a wide gap between the organization's goals and its abilities
- market niches exist that it wishes to enter but is unable to do so effectively
- the product line needs to be expanded

- the organization would benefit from better market recognition
- rationalization of scattered marketing efforts would reduce costs

✓ *Technological Reasons.* It has been determined that:
- another organization has proprietary technology that would be of great benefit
- R&D capability is inadequate
- equipment and technology is outdated
- technologies are changing so fast that the risk of being tied to one area is very high

✓ *Financial Reasons.* The organization needs:
- better cash resources
- to borrow money, or to borrow at a reasonable rate
- a revenue stream that is less dependent on a narrow range of products/services
- to speed up its cash flow
- to leverage its fixed costs
- to improve its return on equity

✓ *Human Resources Reasons.* The organization lacks:
- knowledge and skills for a new area of enterprise
- leadership to take it where it wants to be
- ability to be innovative and creative in appealing new areas

✓ *Service Reasons.* The organization's ability to serve its customers would be enhanced if it were able to:
- strengthen its relationship with key customers by integrating aspects of its business with theirs
- access better channels of distribution
- improve delivery times and on-time ratios to key customers

✓ *Production Reasons.* The organization is suffering because of:
- operating well below full capacity
- a slow production cycle
- inefficient production systems
- high cost of supplies and subcontractors, leaving it at a competitive disadvantage

Partnerships: Going International

The greater the tension, the greater the potential. Great energy springs from a correspondingly great tension of opposites.

—Carl Jung

As the world economy shrinks step-by-step into a united mass, more and more companies consider it imperative to gain a foothold in other markets through acquisitions and strategic partnerships. Here are some principles that will enhance your organization's chances of creating a successful overseas partnership.

✓ Consider using an agent. In an ideal world an organization would want one of its employees working within a partnership organization in another country. This is not always possible for smaller companies or when the size and importance of the overseas partner are less significant. The next best alternative may be a local agent, who:
  • will already be familiar with your partner
  • can make visits frequently and at low cost
  • can intervene in a more culturally sensitive way when roadblocks are encountered

✓ A poor agent, however, can seriously damage your relationship with your partner organization, so ensure that you:
  • do your due diligence to ensure that you recruit someone with an impeccable reputation

- ensure that the agent has no conflict of interest caused by representing other organizations similar to yours
- clearly define your expectations, in writing
- limit the agent's role to day-to-day activities but not in major decisions or strategic issues
- avoid making a long-term commitment until the agent has proved himself

✓ Be prepared to spend a considerable amount of time getting into the heads of the people you are dealing with. Find out everything about their cultures. Are they conservative? In what way? Are they religious? How so, and what philosophy do they follow? What are their time horizons? What do they expect from a westerner? How do they perceive westerners?

✓ Get to know the key people well. Find out about their likes and dislikes, what motivates them, what angers them, how they spend their spare time, their beliefs, and their family lives. By showing interest in key people and modifying your approach to fit their styles, you are more likely to avoid irritants and misunderstandings that can sour a relationship.

✓ Expect to change your behavior to suit that of the potential partners, not the other way around.

✓ Avoid creating an impression that you will deliver more than you are capable of. Ensure that expectations are realistic.

✓ Deal with legal aspects last.

✓ Ensure that your key people are likely to stay with you and help sustain relationships.

✓ Temper your expectations about speedy conclusions to negotiations. Asian and European organizations are much less sensitive about time issues than are North Americans. Getting to know and trust you will be a slow process that cannot be done overnight. So expect to spend longer to reach an agreement and get decisions made than might be the case at home.

✓ Learn about the financial details of your partners' environment. Find out about their tax laws so that you can use them to your advantage. Understand that profit margins are typically lower in countries outside North America, since volume, market penetration, and longer-term success are often more important than short-term profitability.

✓ Be cautious about the currencies used for transacting business. Your controller may have information about the advantages of certain currencies over others, favorable exchange rates, or problems associated with currency conversion.

✓ Authority to negotiate is essential. Ensure that the person or team you are dealing with has the power to conclude a deal. If not, avoid details and key issues until you are face-to-face with the real decision maker.

✓ Be prepared for some give-and-take on benefits. You're in the relationship for the long term; learn to give a little so that you can expect something in return. Giving in on a number of small issues could enable you to win big on major items.

Partnerships:
Managing the Process

A successful marriage is an edifice that must be rebuilt every day.

—Andre Maurois

Before signing a deal to work together it is critical to get to know your prospective partner. Although the chemistry between the leaders on both sides is important, day-to-day relationships will be handled by middle managers. So it is important to set up a joint committee to find out as much as possible about the other organization. Here are some issues for a joint committee to review:

✓ What is the goal of the proposed partnership? What are we trying to achieve? How will we know if we have been successful? How will we measure success?

✓ What is the other organization's goal(s)? Will we be able to meet those expectations? What role do they expect us to play? What responsibility will we have?

✓ How will we manage the relationship? Who will be interfacing with the other organization? Are they compatible? How will it be done? Will we be able to have integrated teams working to assist each other?

✓ Do we have similar business philosophies? Do we speak the same language? Are our organizations and people of a similar level of sophistication?

✔ How will we manage new challenges? When differences and conflicts occur, how will we settle them?

The benefits of this joint investigative committee include:

✔ Getting a firm understanding about each other's level of commitment to working together.
✔ Demonstrating a consultative approach so that future dealings can be handled in an equally collaborative manner.
✔ Highlighting potentially explosive issues so that they can be laid to rest before they can do damage.
✔ Creating a climate of goodwill and camaraderie that, hopefully, will continue.

The joint committee should produce specific deliverables, such as:

✔ A charter of values, guiding principles, and points of consensus, all of which will form the basis of a solid relationship.
✔ Early identification of potential roadblocks to success. If major problems cannot be solved early on, the chances of a lasting and growing alliance are slim.
✔ A game plan to identify and resolve problems and reduce mistakes, waste, and stress later on.
✔ A sense of joint responsibility for results.

Reengineering and Downsizing

Those who have changed the universe have never done it by changing officials,
but by inspiring the people.

—Napoleon

Consultants are a strange breed. They all want to be seen to be on the leading edge of ideas and innovations. A case in point is the concept of reengineering, which some claim was "discovered" in the early 1990s. Nothing could be further from the truth. Industrial engineering schools have been teaching the primary tool of reengineering—process mapping—since the 1920s. What is perhaps different is how widely the concept has been used to change businesses fundamentally instead of tackling isolated processes individually.

Why do organizations exist? To satisfy customers, to provide employment, or to line the pockets of shareholders? The answer surely is all of the above—we need to satisfy all the stakeholders. But everything starts with customer satisfaction, for if we don't do that, we can't fund salaries for employees, or dividends and profits for the shareholders.

How is this best done? Sometimes growing the business is appropriate, but there may be times when we need to pull in the reins. Reengineering and downsizing are two approaches that are similar in some respects and very different in others.

Reengineering is about examining and improving our key work processes. It involves documenting our existing processes and then finding innovative ways of reducing the time they take and improving consistency of results. It requires that we eliminate waste, duplication, and non-value-added activities so that the streamlined process represents a dramatic improvement. It may result in reducing the number of jobs although that is not the objective.

Downsizing is different. It is an approach focused on reducing costs rather than improving services. It typically involves the elimination of jobs and large-scale firing of people. The process is usually done quickly, with little involvement by department managers, and results in immediate short-term cost reduction.

Reengineering requires rethinking how we do business. It is an inclusive process. The benefits are significant, especially for the customer, but also for the owners (lower costs) and employees (less frustration, greater input).

Downsizing can devastate an organization. The benefits are short-lived and the results can be counterproductive:

- ✓ Morale will plummet.
- ✓ Employees will become gun-shy, and innovation and change will dry up.
- ✓ Service levels will decline, as key knowledgeable employees are often eliminated.
- ✓ Costs often go up as we tend to rely more on consultants (often placing previous employees back in an advisory role).
- ✓ Business is lost because of disruptions in operations, requiring additional layoffs.

What's the moral of the story?

- ✓ Think carefully before cutting costs by laying off people.
- ✓ Consider how customers will be affected by employee cutbacks.
- ✓ Pursue alternative strategies to improve the bottom line.

Stakeholders

There can be no real individual freedom in the presence of economic insecurity.
—Chester Bowles

It takes a blend of leader, magician, and politician to find that special balance among competing stakeholders and be able to satisfy them all. Doing so starts with understanding those stakeholders.

✓ Employees

Your employees are probably your most important stakeholders, since their performance will determine whether the customers are satisfied. In turn, the customers will provide your organization with a lever of revenues and margins that will satisfy the shareholders. So what will it take to satisfy employees? There is an abundance of theories and statistics, but most point to the simple fact that people want to feel appreciated, respected, and included. What this means specifically is that people want:

- *Control Over Their Environments*. People want to be able to make decisions or to be consulted when others make decisions that affect them.
- *Information*. People want access to relevant information—they don't want to have to rely on the grapevine for news.
- *Validation*. People want to know how they're doing. They want timely feedback that confirms whether they are meeting or exceeding

expectations. And they appreciate constructive criticism that allows them an opportunity to improve their performance.

- *Learning Opportunities.* This is especially true with the upcoming "chips and pop" generation of younger workers, who are less loyal to organizations and are looking for what they can get out of the employment situation. Few things are more valuable to these workers than skills that are portable and can be applied in the current or an alternative work situation.

✓ Shareholders

Your shareholders are looking for return on capital employed. People who have invested their money in an enterprise typically look for the highest reward possible. This may come in the form of profits, dividends, growth, increased share price/value, or a combination of these factors.

✓ Customers

Whether your organization is a manufacturer, a sales operation, or a service provider, customers have the same basic needs:

- *Quality.* Foremost in the minds of customers, clients, or patients is the desire to receive a product or service that meets—or exceeds—their expectations, the first time and every time. Consistency in product delivery helps ensure that unpleasant surprises never annoy the customer.
- *Speed.* Consumers want transactions to be done quickly and on time. Time is money. Organizations that have streamlined their processes to eliminate delays have a significant advantage over those that have not. Internet, wireless, and other technologies are helping organizations make quantum strides in this area of competitiveness.
- *Empathy.* Consumers want to be dealt with in a caring manner. If there is a problem, it needs to be handled by employees who are

sympathetic, who can see the issues from *the customer's* perspective, and who will try to address customer concerns immediately.

- *Competence.* Customers want to work with employees who are knowledgeable about their products or services and can share their information effectively.
- *Tangibility.* The five senses—sight, touch, taste, hearing, and smell—all generate impressions that are measured against expectations. These include such things as a receptionist's smile, a friendly, lively voice on the telephone, colorful and artistic presentation of products, a fresh-smelling environment, the view from a window, the clarity of ambient music or audiovisuals, or hot drinks and snacks for browsing or waiting customers.
- *Value.* Most customers don't mind paying more if they see value in what they are buying. But they hate to pay more and then feel cheated when they get inferior service or a product that falls below their expectations.

✓ Government

Although many industrial and professional associations lobby on behalf of the organizations or individuals who belong to them, your company may also have to deal directly with government bureaucracies at several levels, from municipal to federal. They have two chief concerns:

- *Compliance.* At a minimum, bureaucrats at all levels of government want corporations to obey the relevant laws, from health and safety regulations to environmental guidelines, from financial reporting requirements to tax remittances—and many more.
- *Responsibility.* Governments want corporations to take the lead in creating jobs, outsourcing opportunities within the community rather than abroad, and paying taxes to support the local economy.

✓ Public

The general public includes a vast variety of concerned citizens, from people who live in the same community as your organization to those in other parts of the world whose environment may be affected by its operations—and, of course, potential customers! This is what they want from you:

- *Generosity.* Rightly or wrongly, members of the public see corporations as generators of large amounts of cash. They expect organizations to invest a percentage of profits in their local communities, for example, providing prizes for local functions, donating to institutions in need, sponsoring kids' teams, or making employees available for United Way campaigns.

- *Good Citizenship.* The public expects corporations to be concerned about the community's health and safety and not to do anything that would affect anyone adversely. No corporation that is truly part of its community would do things such as producing drugs that have been found to be dangerous, spilling toxins into rivers and lakes, exploiting people simply because they have no political power, or allowing unsafe working conditions to go uncorrected.

Strategic Planning

The greatest danger for most of us lies not in setting our aim too high and falling short; but in setting our aim too low and achieving our mark.

—Michelangelo

Imagine yourself behind the wheel of a sports car. You're traveling along a winding road. Where are your eyes? Hopefully they are focusing on the road ahead, at your anticipated route, with only an occasional glances at the rearview mirror.

Leaders are like drivers. They need to spend most of their time looking at the road ahead, trying as best they can to anticipate every turn and pothole. Looking in the rearview mirror too often could spell disaster.

Strategic planning is the purview of senior leaders in an organization, their attempts to predict and influence the future. Its creation is the product of a combined effort of the board and senior management. It is a long and arduous task, but the benefits of a documented strategic plan go well beyond the plan itself to include the discussions that take place as a result of the research, soul-searching, and decision making.

Any reasonable organization is likely to take up to a year to develop a strategic plan if one does not already exist. Those that have been through the process will do one in probably half the time, or less, as they have a framework and a process already in place.

Creating a strategic plan requires stamina, hard work, an open mind, and discipline. These steps will lead planners to the desired outcome:

✓ Call a meeting of a cross-section of senior people with influence and announce your intention. Let them know the purpose, the benefits, and the steps you intend to take to create the plan. Be realistic about the process and the work required, and what you will do with the plan when it is complete.

✓ Create your volunteer team. The team should consist of:
  • representatives of key stakeholders such as employees, the union (if any), and even key customers
  • representatives of major functions and divisions
  • people with complementary skills and personalities

✓ Create a roadmap of the steps you will take to complete the plan. Set a realistic timeline for completion of each major part of the plan.

✓ Get commitment from each of the members to provide regular monthly updates and attend decision-making meetings.

✓ Understand who will be using this plan (for example, board, shareholders, investors, financial institutions, employees). Based on their needs, create a broad outline of the final report. This will give you a good indication of the work to be done. A table of contents will provide the highlights, enabling you to focus on the big picture without getting embroiled in small details.

✓ Next, filter the details further into possible subheadings and possible appendices. Understanding who will be reading the plan will give you a clue as to the level of detail you will be producing.

✓ Prepare the work plan. Decide who will be researching and documenting each section of the report, how they will do it, when it is expected and the resources available (consultants, travel, etc.).

Step 2: Examine and Evaluate the Current Situation

✓ The most common approach is to do a SWOT analysis: strengths, weaknesses, opportunities, and threats. (See Chapter 45, "Strategic Planning: SWOT Analysis.")

✓ Be objective in your analysis. This analysis will bring you to the realization that leading organizations:
  - have a strong cash position, with access to contingency funds
  - are sensibly financed, with a prudent mix of equity and debt
  - have above-average profitability in terms of return on capital invested
  - shoot for rapid growth in revenue
  - target faster-growing market segments
  - develop strong product or service brands
  - devote substantial resources to innovation by encouraging risk taking and research
  - compete on service rather than price
  - work hand-in-glove with customers and respond with lightning speed to their needs
  - attract and retain top people and invest in their development

Step 3: Develop Your Vision

✓ The vision is the dream that the key leaders have for their organizations. It is the goal statement that should inspire employees to strive toward it. It should tug at the heartstrings of those who read it and propel them to join the cause to make it happen.

✓ Creating a compelling vision is no easy task. Knowing whom to involve adds to the complexity. As a general rule, employees look to leadership to provide the vision, although the more mundane mission may involve more rank-and-file people.

✓ Creating a vision takes time. The process can be expedited if you:
  - Consider vision statements from other organizations. Decide what you like about each and what you don't like.

- Put yourself in the position of a visiting alien. If an alien visited your company in, say five years, how would you like the alien to describe your organization?
- Collect ideas and identify key words.
- Have a subcommittee create a draft for everyone to review.
- Fine-tune the draft, making sure that the statement gives a clear sense of the organization in terms of size, physical appearance, and activities. Confirm with key members of the leadership team that each of them buys into the statement.

(See Chapter 49, "Visioning.")

STEP 4: DEVELOP YOUR MISSION

✓ The mission statement describes the nature of the business and how matters are conducted on a day-to-day basis. The mission will be specific enough to give everyone reading it a clear picture of:
- *what* the business does
- *whom* it serves
- *what* it provides
- *how* it does so
- *where* it operates
- *what* benefits accrue to stakeholders

✓ The mission statement is a team effort. It is created with input from senior managers, all of whom have had a chance to contribute their ideas. The process goes more quickly if the following steps are taken:
1. Review the mission statements of a variety of organizations, distinguishing between those that people like and those that they do not.
2. Establish a template for each person to use. The template will identify the key features that are required in the final statement, including the nature of your business, whom you serve, how you serve customers, and the benefits for all stakeholders.

3. Have each person create his own mission statement.
4. Post these statements on the wall for everyone to see.
5. Discuss the statements, identifying those that people like the most. To avoid giving preference by seniority, do not attach names to any of them.
6. Pick the best elements.
7. Have a small team craft a proposed statement from the group's best ideas.
8. Have the whole group approve the draft or modify it so that a general consensus is achieved.

✓ Post the mission statement in a prominent place to make everyone aware of it. Consider having rollout meetings to explain it to employees, why it is important, how they fit in, and their roles in making it a reality. Where possible, have each person sign his or her name on it to symbolize buy-in.

STEP 5: *DEVELOP OBJECTIVES*

✓ Create broad objectives using the information gathered from inside and outside the organization. These will cover the needs of all stakeholders, such as profitability and market share for shareholders, quality of work life for employees, and service excellence for customers. The objectives will also reflect the underlying reasons for running the business.

STEP 6: *REVIEW YOUR VALUES*

✓ Values describe our attitude and behavior toward the operation of the business and its relationships with society at large, customers, suppliers, employees, the local community, and other stakeholders. Many organizations have no documented values. Others have values but they are largely ignored. Either way, the internal research will reveal gaps between how you want to behave and how you do. This should lead to a discussion on the behaviors you expect, which should be documented.

✓ Decide how to ensure that the values are practiced more consistently on a day-to-day basis. You can, for example, build those behaviors into the performance review system so that employees who practice them are rewarded for doing so.

Step 7: Set Goals

✓ Goals are more specific and more time-based than objectives. A simple formula for defining goals is to ensure that they are specific, measurable, agreed upon, realistic (yet challenging), and time-based (SMART).

✓ Goals should be established for factors such as market (size and share), products, finances, profitability, utilization and efficiency, innovation, and learning (people development).

Step 8: Create Strategies and Plans

✓ Generate strategies by which the mission and objectives will be achieved. These can involve the business as a whole, including such matters as diversification, organic growth, or acquisition plans, or they can relate to primary matters in key functional areas. Here are some examples:
  - "The company's internal cash flow will fund all future growth."
  - "New products will progressively replace existing ones over the next three years."
  - "All assembly work will be contracted out to lower the company's break-even point."

✓ Develop a specific plan to achieve each goal. For plans to be achieved in the next twelve months, list the tasks, who will do them, and when they will be done. For medium-term goals, state the quarter during which they should be done. For long-term goals, state the year in which they should become a reality.

STEP 9: DEVELOP INDICATORS TO TRACK CHANGES

✓ Identify indicators to track your progress in categories such as quality/service, timeliness/responsiveness, costs/value, health and safety, and morale.

✓ You should not have more than two indicators in each category. Otherwise you'll spend too much time on data collection, leaving little time for analyzing, planning, and taking corrective action.

✓ Ensure that your chosen indicators relate specifically to the intentions outlined in your mission.

The best indicators in each category will be those that are:

- easy to collect
- accurate
- already being collected
- measurable
- something the team can influence

✓ If you have picked an indicator that is not being measured, set up a data collection system and get your people to take responsibility for collection.

STEP 10: DOCUMENT THE PLAN

✓ When writing the plan:

- avoid unnecessary jargon
- economize on words
- use short, crisp sentences and bullet points
- check spellings
- concentrate on relevant and significant issues
- break the text into numbered paragraphs, sections, etc.
- relegate detail to appendices
- provide a contents page and number the pages
- write the summary *last*

✓ Get a qualified outsider to review your plan in draft form and be prepared to adjust it in the light of his or her comments and experiences. Although outsiders can provide objectivity and assist in fine-tuning the plan, it is essential that they not be permitted to change the recommendations, as the content needs to be owned by the plan's creators.

✓ If presenting the plan to outside stakeholders, ensure that the document has an executive summary, a table of contents, appendices, and numbered pages. Finally, package the report with an attractive cover to give it a professional look.

Strategic Planning: SWOT Analysis

In the business world, the rearview mirror is always clearer than the windshield.

—Warren Buffett

SWOT stands for strengths, weaknesses, opportunities, and threats. Strengths and weaknesses are essentially internal to an organization and relate to matters concerning resources, programs, and organization in key areas. Opportunities and threats tend to be external—from competing organizations, global trends, and other environmental factors. Let us review how both internal and external factors influence a strategic plan.

INTERNAL FACTORS (STRENGTHS AND WEAKNESSES)

As part of this investigation, the planning team may want to ask these questions:

- ✔ Is the current vision being realized? If not, why not?
- ✔ How has the company's focus changed over the past few years? Why have changes occurred (or why not)? Identify primary reasons and categorize them as either internal or external.
- ✔ What strategies have been followed over the past few years in respect to products/services, operations, finance, marketing, technology, management, etc.? Critically examine each strategy statement by questioning activities and actions in key functional areas. For example:

- How have we been managed?
- How are we funded?
- How have we attempted to increase sales and market share?
- How have we performed in terms of productivity and costs?

✓ The process of internal research is challenging in that getting accurate, frank information is essential. There may be an advantage in having a neutral third party conduct focus-group interviews to get to the truth. Focus groups should be made up of a cross-section of employees from all parts of the organization and at all levels. Determine the values that are being practiced in the organization. Use the focus groups to answer such questions as:
- Do we practice what we preach?
- Does senior management act as a good role model?
- What is our attitude toward risk taking?
- How effective are we at communicating?
- To what extent do we respect the opinions of people on the front lines?
- Do we recognize superior effort and performance?
  Failure to practice open communications, to encourage calculated risks, or to involve and recognize employees mean that it's unlikely you'll be able to implement any plan successfully.

EXTERNAL FACTORS (OPPORTUNITIES AND THREATS)

When turning to the outside, determine how effective you are by benchmarking your performance against others inside and outside your industry. A variety of approaches can be adopted in benchmarking performance, all of which have some merit. (See Chapter 29, "Benchmarking.") Look at similar organizations to compare yourself on operating statistics and best practices as well as strengths and weaknesses.

✓ Look beyond your industry at organizations in different industries that have similar processes (sales, purchasing, human resources management, etc.). This may give you the best information, as organizations that are not in competition with you are more likely to share, especially if they learn from you in return. Either way, it is advisable to use your employees rather than a consultant to gather this information, as it adds to the buy-in factor.

✓ Meet with your customers to find out:
- what you do that makes them loyal to you
- what frustrates them when they deal with you
- how user-friendly your customer services are
- what policies prevent people from doing their best

✓ Collect information on the outside forces that will influence you, including:
- what's happening with your main competitors (their strengths and weaknesses)
- current or future changes in legislation that may affect your industry
- economic trends that will have an impact your revenues and costs
- new technologies that might revolutionize how you do business

✓ Review the threats and opportunities. For example:
- your own industry, where structural changes may be occurring (size and segmentation, growth patterns and maturity, established patterns and relationships, emergence/contraction of niches, international dimensions, relative attractiveness of segments)
- the marketplace, which may be changing because of economic or social factors (customers, distribution channels, social/demographic issues, political and environmental factors)
- the competition, which may be creating new threats or opportunities (identities, performance, market share, likely plans, aggressiveness, strengths and weaknesses)
- new technologies, which may be causing fundamental changes in products, processes, etc. (substitute products, alternative solutions, shifting channels, cost savings, etc.)

Sustainability

Human subtlety will never devise an invention more beautiful,
more simple or more direct than does Nature, because in her
inventions, nothing is lacking and nothing is superfluous.
—Leonardo DaVinci

Corporate sustainability is a business approach that creates value by managing and balancing the risks deriving from the economic, environmental, and social aspects of an organization's operations. More organizations than ever before are recognizing the link between sustainable development and business growth. They include global organizations such as British Petroleum P.L.C., Royal Bank of Canada, and Nokia Corporation, which have embraced this new business philosophy by implementing plans for improvement together with measurement and reporting mechanisms.

✓ Corporate sustainability recognizes and accepts that corporate leaders have a choice in how they conduct business operations—that they can actively choose to protect the environment and enhance society without sacrificing profitability.

✓ The concept of operating within strict ethical boundaries can be seen as a response to:

- pressures from the investment community, environmentalists, NGOs, and other stakeholders affected by company operations
- a world where information about global events can be transmitted

instantaneously, enabling interested parties to monitor corporate activities in any corner of the globe

✓ More investors now take into consideration a corporation's commitment to issues such as environmental protection, abolition of child labor, community involvement, and other indicators of a sustainable business approach.

✓ Corporations that fail to expand their indicators of success to include nonfinancial accountability are at risk of failing to win the support of investors, trading partners, employees, and regulatory bodies.

✓ The quality of a company's management of risk deriving from economic, environmental, and social developments can be quantified using tools such as the Global Reporting Initiative (GRI). GRI is a multistakeholder process whose mission is to develop and disseminate sustainability reporting guidelines. Sustainability reports can be used by the investment community to identify and select leading companies.

✓ In quantifying their own sustainability performance, leading organizations are moving to external verification of their reports (such as GRI) to build brand value and enhance stakeholder trust.

✓ One demonstration of commitment to sustainable business development is the move to "triple bottom-line" reporting. Triple bottom-line reporting, or sustainability reporting, is the process of monitoring, measuring, reporting on, and continuously improving performance in three areas: financial responsibility, environmental responsibility, and corporate social responsibility.

✓ By linking profit to principles, business leaders have recognized that financial indicators alone do not adequately reflect their business risks. Measuring, accounting for, and reporting nonfinancial indicators as part of a performance management system allows organizations to safeguard their reputations, build trust among stakeholders, retain investor confidence, and ultimately improve overall corporate performance.

✓ New values have emerged in Western societies that recognize the impact of large commercial operations on the societies in which they operate. Sustainability assessment and reporting should make a corporation's operations more transparent to all stakeholders and provide its leaders with a compass to ensure long-term survival and growth for the benefit of all.

Sustainability: Evaluating Your Organization

Drive thy Business or it will drive thee.

—Benjamin Franklin

Improving an organization's corporate sustainability takes effort. A plan for improvement begins with identification of opportunities (that is, gaps). Here is a checklist that can serve as an initial guide to what needs to be done.

EMPLOYEES

Diversity

Does your organization:

☐ have a documented policy that encourages the hiring of diverse peoples?

☐ have a system to ensure that people of all backgrounds have equal opportunity for promotions?

☐ ensure that disadvantaged people are given the training opportunities necessary to allow them to compete for new opportunities on a level playing field?

Employee Programs

Does your organization:

☐ encourage work/life balance?

☐ have share-ownership programs that are extended beyond executives?

☐ have a commitment to employee development?

☐ provide adequate funding for employee education outside of the workplace?

☐ have programs that provide maternity benefits?

☐ provide time away from work to take care of immediate family crises?

Health and Safety

Does your management:

☐ pay more than lip service to health and safety issues?

☐ ensure that employee concerns are dealt with expeditiously?

☐ track health and safety statistics to ensure continuous improvement?

☐ conduct regular inspections to ensure that planned changes have actually been implemented?

☐ empower all employees to be proactive in dealing with unsafe working conditions?

☐ regularly communicate its concern about health and safety to employees?

☐ promote and fund proactive wellness programs?

Labor Relations and Unions

Does your management:

☐ respect its relationship with its bargaining unit?

☐ collaborate on issues of mutual concern?

☐ avoid engaging in anti-union rhetoric?

Human Rights

Does your management:

☐ have a policy that enshrines the rights of all employees, irrespective of race, country of origin, ethnicity, sexual orientation, or gender, to freedom from harassment as well as equal opportunity?

☐ deal swiftly and decisively with issues of harassment?

The Community and Larger Society

Does your organization:

☐ encourage employees to be actively involved in community projects?

□ donate a fixed percentage of its income to charitable causes?

□ engage the public in decisions that might affect the community?

□ modify decisions based on the outcome of this consultation?

□ have a policy against bribery and illegal influence of buyers and politicians?

□ avoid making statements or claims that are inaccurate or misleading in any way?

□ immediately withdraw products that may have an adverse impact on the health and welfare of their users?

□ engage and work collaboratively with native communities when the organization's actions may be seen to have an impact on their lives?

CUSTOMERS

Does your organization:

□ continuously collect data on levels of customer satisfaction?

□ put focused effort into correcting issues relating to customer complaints?

□ reward employees according to customer satisfaction, whether customers are internal or external?

□ discipline employees who may have damaged relationships with customers?

□ make efforts to establish long-term relationships with customers?

CORPORATE GOVERNANCE

Does your organization:

□ have an independent board of directors?

□ separate the role of chairperson of the board and CEO?

□ have a documented code of ethics?

□ have a statement of values?

□ continuously reward employees for operating according to these ethics and values and disciplining those who do not?

□ reward executives for performance based on goal attainment rather than share-price improvement?

☐ compensate senior employees reasonably in relation to salaries of the lowest-paid people in the organization?

☐ have board committees, such as audit, risk management, and compensation, with independent directors?

ENVIRONMENT

Does your management:

☐ have a formal environmental protection program?

☐ have certification (ISO 14000) for its practices?

☐ allocate responsibility for managing, measuring, and improving environmental management practices?

☐ measure, monitor, and provide feedback to employees on changes in its level of achievement?

☐ set targets for continuous improvement?

☐ benchmark your practices against industry leaders?

☐ encourage employees to make efficient use of energy and water?

☐ monitor and help reduce emissions, discharge, and spills?

☐ encourage biodiversity and effective use of land?

☐ measure its effectiveness in terms of reducing and/or preventing penalties, fines, convictions, and incidents of noncompliance?

Unions

We formed our union because we could not depend on employers to provide us with dignity, a measure of security and a rising standard of living.
—Canadian Auto Workers Union, Web Site Statement of Principles

Having a unionized workforce is often considered about as rewarding as eating glass. This is because managers tend to treat the union as the enemy rather than as an important stakeholder.

Why is there a union representing your employees? At some stage in your organization's history, people may not have been treated as well as they should have been. Wages and benefits may have been below average; perhaps working conditions were poor or safety was an issue. That was a mistake, and one that had consequences that will have to be lived with for a long time. It is important to learn to live with your union in a mutually satisfactory relationship, because it is highly unlikely that it will be decertified once it has been established.

Management's relationship with the union will be effective for both parties only if it incorporates many of the principles that make for a successful marriage: never take your partner for granted, always spend time talking about issues to make sure there are no misunderstandings, find a balance between giving and taking, and always listen to ensure that you are on track.

Some executives have discovered the formula for successful labor relations. Their companies continue to thrive, much like any other non-union shop that takes care of its people.

During the Life of the Collective Agreement

✓ Treat your union executives as strategic partners, because that is what they are. ("Keep your friends close; keep your enemies closer.")

✓ Understand your collective agreement and, most importantly, make sure that all managers do too. It is the manager's job to run the organization, not the union's. There is unlikely to be anything in a contract that would contravene this, although some overzealous stewards might want the managers to believe that they are the only conduit for information between senior management and the frontline workers.

✓ Respect the letter and spirit of the contract at all times.

✓ Train all managers how to work with the contract. Ensure that at all times they behave in a way that will ensure there is as little disruption as possible. Managers need to be encouraged to:

- be consistent in their dealings with employees
- be consistent in expecting everyone to meet and exceed minimum standards
- deal with issues on their merits
- treat each person with respect and dignity
- not play favorites
- never make allowances for inappropriate or inadequate performance that could be seen as precedents that others will follow

When the Collective Agreement Expires

✓ Labor relations around the time of negotiations are typically more trying. Do everything you can to avoid poisoning attitudes through unnecessarily provocative behavior.

✓ Don't expect your labor-relations negotiators to be gladiators. Know what you require from the bargaining process in order to be competitive in the marketplace. Then expect them to negotiate to get the best deal for the organization. However, the best deal is not necessarily the cheapest deal. You don't want to win the battle but lose the war, as it will likely continue in the trenches. Resentment stemming from an unfair contract will be experienced in many forms: higher absenteeism, grievances, pilferage, and lower productivity. Benefits will be derived when negotiators strive for win-win situations At the same time, realize that an overgenerous deal will affect your organization for years to come, as it will be very difficult to claw back benefits in future negotiations.

✓ Before going into negotiations assess your situation fully.

- Understand what type of union you have. Unions come in all shapes and sizes and can usually be also assessed as left- or right-wing. The more left-wing it is, the more likely it will resist productivity improvement initiatives *unless it has equal control over the design and implementation* of the project. How militant is your union? What has your history with it been like? Is it part of a large international union that could provide the resources to sustain a long strike, or is your organization so small that the larger unions would not want to bother with you?

- Understand how much power you have. What would be the consequences of a strike or lockout? Could you afford it? If so, for how long? How would it affect your customers and your reputation? Could management run the organization without the unionized employees?

- What is your philosophy about replacement workers, if they are allowed? How would the union view your requests in terms of that philosophy? Indeed, are your needs compatible with that philosophy?

- Understand the issues that will be on the table and which of them will be key (they will include nonmonetary items). Understand how any changes in those issues will affect your operations.

✓ Get to know the key people you will be negotiating with. Never begin a negotiation until you understand the other side and their motivations. Who are they? Why are they influential? What are their attitudes toward management? How self-confident are they? Do they carry through with threats? What kind of reputation do they have? Have they led many strikes, or do they tend to "cave" at the eleventh hour? Are they amenable to side deals in spite of all the posturing and pouting around the table?

✓ When the bargaining ends and a deal is struck, how will you know that you've done as well as you can? The answer is when both you and the union have exhausted any power you have, and to go further would be self-destructive for both parties. At that point each party may be able to pull the trigger and force a strike or a lockout, but both are unwilling to do so. The parties have resolved most issues, and on the key issues they were close enough that some compromise was possible.

Visioning

Cherish your visions and your dreams, as they are the children
of your soul; the blueprints of your ultimate achievements.

—Napoleon Hill

A vision and mission are different. The vision is the compelling dream that the leaders create to motivate and challenge the organization. The mission, on the other hand, is a pragmatic statement of what it takes, each day, to move the organization closer to the vision.

Having the ability to formulate a clear, compelling vision and working constantly to achieve it can be a major factor in differentiating between the success and failure of an organization. The vision will create the stimulus and energy to drive performance to ever higher levels.

✓ A vision needs to inspire those who hear or read it. For a vision to be compelling, it must be:
  • short and to the point
  • inspiring
  • connected to the key stakeholders, especially the employees

✓ Avoid creating a vision that's so simplistic it becomes a cliché. Such vision statements talk about being the biggest or best in the world (often interpreted as "most profitable"). They seldom connect with the employees of the organization, whose job it is to make it happen!

Leaving employees out of the vision gives the impression that shareholders are Number One and customers are Number Two, or vice versa. But employees are certainly only Number Three.

✓ Create the vision. This is difficult, and it cannot happen overnight. You need to think about it, dream about it, discuss it, and discover it. Visit companies you admire. Speak to people who have created a legacy. Read about the best. Finally, before putting pen to paper or fingers to keyboard, draw a picture of what your organization should look like, not what it is now—get some crayons and be a kid again. Just draw the images that come to mind and that give you a charge. Take no more than three to five minutes. Then try and put words to the shapes and images you have drawn. Massage those words, time and time again, until they excite you and capture your enthusiasm.

✓ Document the vision. Don't wait for it to percolate upward. But should it come from the leader or the leadership team or be based on a consensus of all employees? Involving frontline employees is impractical in most circumstances. It is up to the leader and his/her team to create it, communicate it, and plan to achieve it.

PART 4

Leading Your People

He who speaks without modesty will find it difficult to make his words good.
—Confucius

Few people today expect to work in a hierarchy that will reward and look after them for life. Many have been victims of downsizing or reorganization, which has engendered a cynical attitude toward the workplace. Most now place their own needs above those of the organization and care more for shorter-term benefits such as training, flexible work hours, and immediate cash bonuses. These same people—not the machines, computers, or buildings—will make or break an organization, as they are the ones who take care of customers and enable organizations to meet their goals.

Most managers repeat the mantra that people are their most important resources, but few frontline employees get a sense that they really are important. Many feel insecure in the knowledge that at the slightest downturn they will be laid off. Also, most organizations spend pitifully few dollars on the development of their people, and they look at those dollars as an expense rather than an investment.

Chapters 50 through 61 will give leaders the tools to turn employees into high-quality workers whose dedication to the organization and its goals are unquestioned. This knowledge will enable organizations to gain a competitive advantage by creating the essential ingredients for success—confident, competent people, superior intellectual capital, and organizational effectiveness.

Abusive Behavior

Forget injuries, but never forget kindness.

—Confucius

The obligations of leadership in an organization go far beyond ensuring a profitable outcome. Indeed, the process of getting there is as important as the end result, for if the process is flawed, so too will be the final outcome.

Abusive leaders are destructive in their behaviors, and they are not easily rehabilitated. They enjoy success and take all the credit while looking to blame others when performance has not met expectations. The atmosphere of command and control is maintained by intimidation.

Some organizations tolerate or even encourage abusive behavior, seeing it as a get-tough strategy to raise performance. And, indeed, sometimes signs of changed behavior appear immediately, but the change is likely to be short-term. Over the longer term, the cost to the organization is likely to be high and will include:

✓ low employee morale, which in turn will result in lower productivity
✓ limited employee input in difficult situations, resulting in poor decisions and low levels of commitment
✓ hidden mistakes, with the resulting "blame game" destroying employees' self-esteem and confidence
✓ high employee turnover, leading to expensive recruiting and training and disruption to customer service
✓ higher levels of sick leave and stress leave
✓ lawsuits against the company for harassment

✓ low levels of creativity and innovation (no matter how smart employees are, they will be unlikely to challenge the status quo, as seen through the eyes of the abuser)

IF YOU SUSPECT THAT YOUR OWN BEHAVIOR IS ABUSIVE

✓ Get help. Find a professional who will be honest with you and can work you through the issues to change your behavior. An appropriate professional will be someone with a counseling background who is capable of winning your confidence, diagnosing the issues, and working with you on behavioral changes.

✓ Get objective feedback on your performance. Undertake a 360-degree evaluation of your impact in the organization by enlisting a sample of at least five people who are likely to tell you how things are rather than what you might want to hear. Expect no mercy, as the process is confidential. Then have a professional provide you with feedback so that you can evaluate your strengths and weaknesses. Create a plan that will enable you to slowly and systematically change the way you interact with others.

✓ Meet with your key people and admit to your sins. This is a major step and will probably be the hardest thing you have ever done in your life. Tell them:
- why you have taken the steps that you have
- what you've discovered about yourself
- what actions you intend to take to make improvements

Ask for their help in making the situation better. Invite them to give you feedback on your progress.

✓ Take some courses to help provide you with tools that will make you a better listener, more humble, and capable of empowering others.

✓ Monitor your progress by observing the things you do and the reaction from others, as well as from the feedback you solicit from employees and your coach.

✓ Reward yourself by celebrating positive changes. Treat yourself to little luxuries that will reinforce the efforts you have made.

IF YOUR MANAGER IS ABUSIVE

✓ Be realistic about your chances of changing him or her.

✓ Assess whether your manager is there for the short or the long term. If it's the former, you may want to wait it out in the hope that he will be fired or leave sooner rather than later. (A clue to the possible length of stay is the person's past record of employment.)

✓ Consider looking for another job. If you feel that the abuser will stick around and has the support of influential people—for example, on the board—then you need to be realistic. Either look for opportunities outside the organization or try to find a way of working around that person.

IF YOU HAVE AN ABUSER REPORTING TO YOU

✓ Meet with the abuser to confront her about the issue. Be well prepared, since you can expect a hostile response and denial. Be frank, pointing out specific examples from what you have observed. Let her know the consequences of her behavior for the organization. Appeal to her commitment to the organization to correct the situation. If she refuses to acknowledge the problem, point out the serious consequences that lack of change will have on her career and the likely steps that will result.

✓ Take the person out of a managerial role into an advisory, consultative, or technical role. The more power you can strip him of, the better.

✓ Meet with the team who reported to the abuser. Deal with the topic professionally. Do not dwell on personalities, although you should acknowledge the problems. Ask the group for suggestions as to how the situation can best be turned around.

✓ Before taking drastic action consult with your human resource department to review the case and evaluate your options.

Coaching

SIGN POSTED IN A VOLUNTEER CENTER FOR THE ELDERLY
If you want happiness for an hour, take a nap.
If you want happiness for a day, go fishing.
If you want happiness for a year, inherit a fortune.
If you want happiness for a lifetime, help someone else.

—Unknown

Coaching for skills development is based on the same principles that underlie all effective coaching:

- ✔ a formal (or implied) contract about the objective, with two-way expectations and boundaries
- ✔ observable behavior as a foundation for feedback
- ✔ feedback that balances positive reinforcement with suggestions for improvement
- ✔ opportunities for demonstration and practice
- ✔ measures and standards of success
- ✔ benefits for the individual and the organization

Managers coach for skill development to support formal training or on-the-job training. The objective of coaching is to increase an employee's confidence and success in his current role or to prepare the employee for greater responsibilities in other roles.

These are the benefits of one-on-one coaching for skills development:

✓ Coaching is targeted to the employee's experience level and role in the organization.

✓ It can be conducted over several sessions.

✓ Assumptions can be probed and tested.

✓ Employees can practice new skills immediately and receive prompt feedback.

✓ Both parties can discuss their preferred feedback styles and create a two-way feedback agreement.

✓ Success can be recognized and rewarded immediately.

Here are some practical guidelines for leaders to follow in coaching situations.

✓ Provide the employee with an overview of the business plan to show how her work fits into the bigger picture.

✓ When setting a plan, establish some visible measures for success to give you a benchmark for your input.

✓ Solicit the employee's perspective on his current level of performance.

✓ Do some two-way brainstorming about practical assignments for applying new skills.

✓ Refer the employee to specific internal courses, when appropriate, to support your one-on-one coaching.

✓ Solicit the employee's input about the nature and frequency of follow-up meetings and what feedback is required.

✓ When suggesting improvements or next steps, focus first on the desired outcome and then on the improvement.

✓ Identify others in the organization who can act as role models for the specific skills you are addressing.

✓ Be sure to address the *when* and *why* as well as the *how* and *what* in coaching sessions.

✓ Reward skill development with creative assignments that balance risk taking and confidence building.

✓ As employees master new skills, arrange for them to coach others, thus sustaining and reinforcing their development.

Compensation and Benefits

Money is better than poverty, if only for financial reasons.
—Woody Allen

The governance model requires that we move away from oligarchic corporate structures. These fiefdoms often enable egotistical, greedy CEOs to loose touch with people on the front line while creating featherbeds for themselves— sometimes translating into compensation packages that are 200 to 500 times as much as those of their frontline workers.

As a leader, you understand that the salaries and benefits you provide your people sends a message about how much you value people. If you truly believe that people are your most important resource and that the talents of most people are underutilized, you need to compensate them accordingly.

Paying money to employees may not be sufficient to buy their love or loyalty, but it is clearly necessary to attract, motivate, and retain the requisite talent. Adequate compensation is something that causes either more or less satisfaction. It is generally recognized that few people leave an organization because of the pay. More often they leave because of a poor relationship with their immediate bosses. As a leader your task is not to design the compensation and benefits plan but to provide the philosophy and guiding principles that will influence its design.

✓ No amount of money or benefits will produce a motivated, productive workforce in the absence of effective relationships between managers and their direct reports. In designing or revising a compensation and benefits plan for employees, leaders should ask themselves these tough questions:

- *Who are our employees?* Have they worked only in the era of daily downsizing, reorganization, and "rightsizing," making them skeptical of management's long-term plans? Do they see themselves more as free agents, motivated by short-term rewards and opportunities for advancement and learning rather than long-term pension benefits? A more mature and stable workforce will appreciate and value longer-term benefits, whereas younger, more-transient workers might be motivated by immediate rewards. The same goes for benefits such paid holidays, access to gymnasiums, day care, medical benefits, and pensions. Younger people may enjoy benefits such as longer holidays and subsidized health and fitness programs, whereas older workers might prefer better pension and retirement programs.

- *What does the future hold for our business?* Are you in a steady industry that rolls along year after year and values long-term retention of people? Or are you in an industry where time horizons are short, technology changes by the day, and people's expectations for longevity in a job are low? If that is so, then short-term incentives would be better than long-term rewards.

- *What are our values?* What kinds of behaviors are you trying to encourage? Do you value risk taking or stability? Does your plan reflect those values? Ask yourself if your existing plan is compatible with the values that your senior leadership team espouses. If not, consider revision based on your ability to fund that change. If your values place a great emphasis on building and retaining intellectual capital, then design a program that will provide rewards in the longer term. If, on the other hand, your business horizons are shorter, adjust the rewards structure so that people will see benefits earlier.

- *Do we need to provide incentives?* There are many different compensation schemes: base pay, variable pay schemes (bonuses or incentives in addition to base pay), and so on. The philosophy behind each scheme is different. Compensation must always be tailored to the respective business needs and prevailing local market conditions. Compensate in a way that supports the goals of your organization and reinforces what you want your employees to achieve. If incentives are important, ask yourself whether your base pay reflects average performance—that is, showing up for work and doing the job as expected. If superior performance is important, have you given employees an opportunity to share in the rewards (and risks) if targets are exceeded?

- *What is the norm in our industry?* Subscribe to industry salary surveys. Share generalities of the information with employees so that they are knowledgeable too. Beware of being too specific in case you are unable to pay industry averages, as this will lead to serious discontent. Do everything you can to ensure that nonmonetary satisfiers make employees feel that management cares about them in other ways.

✓ Design your program to reflect the needs of your employees, your industry, and your values. These may be some of your options:

- If your philosophy is to encourage a collaborative environment, ensure that some percentage of the rewards employees receive is based on the performance of their teams or departments as opposed to individual rewards. Consider a gain-sharing program so that all employees can benefit from improvements in productivity or profits.
- If bonuses are paid, ensure that employees understand why and what their roles were in achieving the additional pay. Set clear goals and expectations around the portion of compensation that is variable. Employees should be rewarded based on measures they can influence through their efforts and authority. (There is nothing worse than dangling a carrot that is neither realistic nor achievable.)
- Consider share options or stock ownership for senior employees if

the market climate is such that the shares are likely to steadily increase in value.

- Be fair. Treat people equally. Make every effort to pay equally for work of equal value. Consider using a job evaluation system that will help you establish a value for the many different types of jobs in your organization. Such a system will help you determine the value of a job in terms of both internal equity and market comparison. Then communicate, communicate, communicate, so that everyone understands the system!

- Make every effort to distinguish between compensation and recognition. The latter consists of one-time rewards for specific achievements that may or may not be repeated, whereas salaries and benefits represent the leaders' obligations to take care of the basic needs of employees. They are unrelated to motivation.

- If recognition is not separated psychologically from compensation, employees will expect it to be repeated. They will become discouraged if similar achievements are not acknowledged in a similar fashion. In fact, it is advisable to recognize individual efforts in nonmonetary ways, with anything from a sincere thank-you to token gifts, meals, and the like.

- Provide the best benefits you can afford. Good benefits are expected as part of a compensation package and are rarely considered a motivator although they may be considered a value that might prevent someone from "jumping ship." They may not give a significant competitive advantage in attracting top talent, but providing good benefits demonstrates that you care. A system of optional benefits to suit your people is a smart way to go. These benefits can range from health and dental plans, to paid leave, flextime, subsidized day care, and a cafeteria, to generous vacations and sports club memberships. What you provide should be consistent with what you and your organization value and the interests of your employees.

✓ Communicate your compensation and benefit plan in as many ways as possible, because misunderstandings are likely to occur. Hold meetings to share the information, especially if it is complicated or offers the employee many options, and supplement the information with easy-to-understand documentation.

• Be cautious when changing the structure of your compensation and benefits program. Making changes can create a minefield. Expect to get few accolades for improvements and significant negativity about real or perceived cutbacks. Hence, the need to communicate openly, honestly, and frequently is critical when any changes to compensation are made. It is vital to listen and respond to concerns and questions.

Inspiring Others

Leaders establish the vision for the future and set the strategy for getting there;
they cause change. They motivate and inspire others to go in the right direction
and they, along with everyone else, sacrifice to get there.

—John Kotter

Along with every leadership role you take comes the opportunity to inspire your followers. This opportunity is not taken by every leader. If you think of the leaders you've admired in the past, it's likely that you found them inspiring.

What exactly does it mean to inspire others? It means creating conditions that cause people around you to feel excited and energized about being part of your team. Although you can't "install" inspiration in others, you can plant the seeds and create the right conditions for it to grow.

Your company can pay your employees to use their minds and bodies on the job, but it is only when they are inspired that their hearts and souls will also be engaged. People who are inspired work longer, harder, faster, and with more enthusiasm than you (or they) might have thought possible. Here's how to be an inspiring leader.

✓ Inspire by example.
  • Be clear and enthusiastic about your own life purpose and goals. The most inspiring leaders are themselves inspired and excited about the purpose of their lives or their missions. Do you know what yours is? If not, consider what you believe is your primary focus, mission, or "calling" in life. Can you articulate this mission in a few simple

words? Do you feel inspired when you express it to others? Sharing your excitement is often a catalyst for others to join in the pursuit of that mission or to find their own, equally inspiring purposes.

- Share stories from your own experience. People who capture the hearts of others and leave them feeling uplifted often do so by sharing stories about their own struggles, mistakes, and life lessons. Be willing to share the human, fallible side of your life experience rather than trying to maintain the façade of a perfect leader who never has doubts or struggles.

- Focus on the dreams and goals of others. If you think about the people you have found inspiring in your own life, it's likely that those people took the time to talk with you and listen to your dreams, goals, and frustrations. They were probably much less focused on what they wanted and much more focused on what others wanted. Get to know your employees and other people with whom you regularly interact. Find out what they want to achieve. Ask what you can do to help. Use your influence to make things happen that make life better for everyone, not just yourself. Adopt a service mindset. Do this not only because it will motivate others to work longer, harder, or faster, but because you truly care about their well-being.

✓ Create and communicate a clear, positive, inclusive vision of the goals to be achieved by your team. People are unlikely to be inspired in situations where they don't know or understand what goals they are working toward or they don't feel their efforts matter much.

- Ensure that you are clear about the goals that have been assigned to your team by management above you. Communicate these goals to your people and listen carefully to their feedback.

- Have the team develop plans for achieving these goals. Ensure that everyone has an opportunity to participate and contribute to the plan, which will encourage buy-in by all members.

- Help others to bring out the best in themselves. Identify the unique

talents and abilities of your employees and ensure that they understand how they can contribute to the overall plan and vision.

- Keep the vision front and center. When things seem to be going off
track and people are losing their focus, remind the team of what
they are working toward.
- Commit to communicating employees' concerns to upper management if something seems confusing or unworkable. Even better, have
your boss join the next employee meeting to hear their concerns
face-to-face.

Knowledge Management: Managing Intellectual Capital

Information and knowledge are the thermonuclear competitive
weapons of our time.
—Thomas A. Stewart, *Intellectual Capital: The New Wealth of Organizations*

As a leader it is your responsibility to understand the value that employees bring to the organization. Leading-edge organizations invest in the development of people to enable them to contribute as much as they are able—intellectually, emotionally, and physically. And they work hard at retaining good people, knowing that resignations represent a brain drain and loss of their investments.

Any successful business strategy should have intellectual capital as its foundation. Even in the most mature industries, companies attempt to differentiate themselves on the basis of some element of intellectual capital. And those that do it best can see the results in terms of patents, copyright ideas, new innovations, and speedy responses.

As a leader, learn to lever the talents of your people more effectively.

✓ Build the philosophy that recognizes people as an asset.
  • Acknowledge that knowledge is people-based, that it is information that has been processed, analyzed, distilled, and packaged by the human mind.
  • Think of your people as gold, and mine their wisdom enthusiastically. Human cognition converts data, information, and knowledge

into wisdom. Most of what your employees know is hidden, because we usually don't know what we know and we don't know who knows it.

- Recognize intellectual capital in its broadest sense, which includes patents, processes, management skills, technologies, information about customers and suppliers, and street smarts.

✓ Create an open environment to encourage knowledge sharing and collaborative pursuit of knowledge.

✓ Differentiate between knowledge and information. Failure to do so will cause you to fall into the technology trap. Information is not knowledge. Knowledge is information that has been transformed into something useful and understandable after being sorted, categorized, and summarized.

✓ Manage knowledge as an asset, the same way that you would take care of financial and physical assets. Measure it. Display its measures (indicators) and make people aware of changes. Celebrate improvements and investigate stagnant or declining performance.

✓ Document knowledge so that it is easily accessible. A knowledge worker processes information and converts it into real value. Organizational knowledge that has been documented is often only a fraction of the knowledge available. So, the more documentation, the greater the ability to use and lever knowledge.

Set up a cross-functional task force to investigate your effectiveness in knowledge management.

✓ Have the task force start the process by documenting your organization's knowledge in three areas:
  1. *Product Knowledge*. Thorough knowledge of the products a supplier manufactures can be leveraged to create value for its customers. In addition, a supplier can differentiate itself by experience gained in cost-effective manufacturing processes.

2. *Process Knowledge.* A common process-knowledge strategy is to pursue low-cost-producer status for a particular technology. Few, if any, processes are seamless. Most contain duplications, delays, and redundant activities. A manufacturer skilled in process design can eliminate these extraneous operations to lower the overall manufacturing cost, as well as reduce cycle time, to gain a significant advantage over competitors.

3. *Customer Knowledge.* Understanding the customer's needs and problems requires sharp listening and observation skills. Innovative problem solving that offers value-added products and services gives any organization a competitive advantage. Most customers value the opportunity to work with suppliers who offer close, multiple contact points within their organizations so that things are accomplished with no hassle.

✓ At the same time, the task force should get answers to the following questions:
- Do your leaders:
  - understand and value the concept of knowledge management?
  - lead by example in promoting the concept?
  - recognize that managing organizational knowledge is central to their business strategies?
  - understand the revenue-generating potential of the organization's knowledge assets and develop strategies for marketing and selling them?
  - use learning to support existing core competencies?
  - hire, evaluate, and compensate recruits based on their potential contributions to your bank of knowledge?
- Does your organization's culture:
  - encourage open and friendly sharing of information?
  - leverage knowledge so that improvements are multiplied across the organization?
  - nurture a climate of openness and trust?

- promote and reward customer-focused, value-added activities?
- encourage employees to take responsibility for their own learning?
- have learning plans that allow all employees to acquire knowledge in the way most meaningful to them?
- Are you using technology to:
  - create a "bank" where you have a good idea of who knows what and who needs to know more?
  - link people to one another and to all relevant external stakeholders?
  - create an institutional memory that is accessible to all employees?
  - bring the organization closer to its customers?
  - foster the development of user-friendly information technology?
  - support collaboration among employees and among departments?
  - systematically organize and transfer knowledge internally?
- Do you measure your knowledge-management processes so that the organization:
  - can link knowledge to financial results?
  - has a specific set of measurable indicators to manage knowledge, which may include copyright materials and patents?
- Do you have processes that:
  - transfer best practices, including documentation and lessons learned?
  - encourage employees to look for ideas in both traditional and nontraditional places?
  - invite outsiders to provide knowledge, as opposed to listening to internal prophets?
  - identify knowledge gaps and use well-defined processes to close them?
  - gather intelligence in a sophisticated and ethical manner?

✓ Based on the lessons learned from your audit, take steps to bring about improvements. A different task force would be useful for making suggestions, but line managers need to be accountable for implementation. Typical postaudit actions include:

- Appointing a chief knowledge officer (CKO) to champion this organizational transformation. Such people are most effective if placed at a sufficiently high level to ensure that their functions are seen as important.
- Allocating sufficient resources toward efforts that measurably increase your knowledge base.
- Ensuring that specialized knowledge is more widely spread. Create protégés to understudy people who have unique skills and knowledge to ensure that these assets are not lost in the event of a resignation.
- Improving sharing through more open communications. Sharing is essential, but it is sometimes difficult to implement in a culture that permits hoarding and hiding of knowledge. The simplest way of ensuring that knowledge is shared and spread is to:
  - Dismantle knowledge storehouses that are typical of silo-type organizational structures. This often requires painful changes, including reorganizing around processes, not functions.
  - Measure and reward information sharing, carefully balancing monetary and other traditional incentives with recognition of the intrinsic value of teamwork and knowledge sharing.
- Setting up measures so that you can track changes. Review these measures regularly at senior management meetings to demonstrate your interest in and commitment to improved knowledge management. Typical indicators include:
  - percentage of employees involved in mentor-protégé activities
  - percentage of employees involved in cross-functional problem-solving teams
  - number of new innovations per period
  - turnaround time to evaluate new suggestions
  - the extent (audited) to which documentation is current
- Using electronic technology to foster increased information sharing, then motivating people to use it, to share their best-practice think-

ing, and to populate it. Technology is such a vital player that leaving it until later would be just as fatal as letting it dominate the initiative.

- Documenting key procedures so that problems can be highlighted and removed. Converting knowledge into intellectual capital requires some degree of formalization. Communicate the streamlined processes to all users, with encouragement not only to use them but also to continuously search for ways to improve them.

- Aligning and optimizing the entire business around delivering that value stream. This extends from the type of customers and opportunities that a sale pursues through to determining appropriate staffing levels in the plant.

- Identifying the core competencies of the company today. Leveraging intellectual capital is more feasible if it is built on the existing strengths of the company. Clues to core competencies may be found in the successful projects and what made them effective. Asking additional questions, such as "What do the customers really need now and what will they need in the future?" and "How do the customers make money, and for what are they willing to pay?" may also reveal opportunities for capturing value with intellectual capital.

- Protecting the knowledge you own. The biggest challenge with intellectual capital is that it is easy to lose or give away. Strategies to protect intellectual capital must be developed not only to protect it from competitors, but also to ensure that it is not given away free to customers either.

- Avoiding laying off your most important employees. If you have no choice but to downsize, be sure to protect the core of your intellectual capital. You have to differentiate between the people who make a real difference in your organization and those who add little value. You must protect those core individuals from leaving and sharing their wisdom—your investment—elsewhere.

Leadership Development: Creating New Leaders

Leadership is about developing leaders, not followers.

—Peter Block

Leadership is about creating a legacy, one that will propel the organization to new levels of success even when the leader has moved on. Many leaders find this difficult to imagine. They are irreplaceable. They have the experience. They know the secrets of success. And they have the intuition that will drive success because their decision making has been fine-tuned over the years.

As wonderful as this vision may seem, it falls short in a world that begs for a new style. Employees are more interested and impressed by someone who listens more than tells, someone who is less concerned about being in charge than about enabling capabilities and outcomes. This vision looks to the style of a leader who recognizes the value of people and the intellectual capital that they are capable of contributing. Working with the human resources and training staff of your organization, here's how you as a leader can create other leaders.

✓ Identify the core competencies for every level of employee in the organization. Research behaviors that will drive the business and emphasize them in selecting training programs and in criteria for judging effectiveness in performance reviews.

✓ Create a training plan for each employee. The most important part of the annual review is a discussion about the future of the employee's career. Central to this discussion should be the creation of a training plan, backed by adequate financing. A leader demonstrates the importance of learning by following up on these plans.

✓ Understand that each person learns differently and that employees need to have tailored learning plans that suit their learning styles. There are many theories of learning, each of which probably has value. Some useful and well-known approaches include:

- Catering to a person's most appropriate sense, whether it's auditory, visual, or kinesthetic. For example, a hands-on person who likes to try things out (kinesthetic) would derive little benefit from a lecture (auditory).

- Allowing people to take varying amounts of responsibility for their own learning, depending on how self-directed they are. Self-directed learners are better able to work on their own, for example, doing training on the Web or their own research. Less self-directed people need more structure and guidance, and would benefit from more formal classroom training.

✓ Encourage people to take responsibility for their own careers. Leaders encourage and enable others to grow and learn—but they don't do it for them. They need to encourage employees to take the initiative and plan their own careers and training, giving feedback only if they are unrealistic or extending their plans beyond reasonable guidelines.

✓ Find the future leaders and focus resources on them. Not everyone wants to be a leader. Nor can everyone become one. So identify those who would benefit most from your time and interest by looking for people who:

- Have a propensity to lead. These people tend to start new initiatives, make the first move, take charge, earn the respect of their peers, and take calculated risks to get things done.

- Bring out the best in others. They are good listeners. They are respectful of different opinions. They are influenced by sound arguments. They treat others with dignity and caring.

Leadership Development: Developing Learning Plans

Teachers open the door. But you must enter by yourself.

—Chinese Proverb

Creating development plans for your employees sends a powerful message that you are promoting their growing abilities to make a contribution to the organization. An Individual Learning Plan is a formal contract between a manager and an employee that identifies specific development activities that link the employee's interests and skills to organizational needs. Learning activities may be both formal and informal and can include self-directed activities, mentoring opportunities, and challenging assignments.

✓ A learning plan is predicated on two-way commitment:
  - the employee's responsibility to do realistic self-assessment and research
  - the manager's responsibility to create a forum for effective discussion and recommendations

✓ The plan is the outcome of one or more meetings that address:
  - the employee's and manager's perspective on the employee's effectiveness in her current role
  - mutual suggestions for increasing impact in the current role

- the employee's longer-term career interests within the organization (typically a two-year view)
- the manager's perspective on preparing for future opportunities, including an overview of organizational priorities
- mutual brainstorming about formal and informal learning opportunities that will lead to improved performance
- agreements about timelines, suggested resources, feedback commitments, and "check-in" dates

Many people benefit from individual development plans.

✓ Employees benefit because:
- ownership for learning and career management rests with the employee primarily
- they are responsible for reflecting on and communicating their own interests, skills, and achievements to their managers
- they can volunteer for participation in satisfying assignments, special projects, and learning activities
- they can relate personal goals to the bigger picture of the organization's long-term business plan
- they can seek feedback about specific development needs and interests
- they can connect with others in the organization, through their managers, who can provide career information and advice

✓ Managers benefit because they can:
- share the responsibility for developmental planning with employees rather than assuming full responsibility
- get a clearer picture of employees' interests and goals and relate those interests to new tasks and assignments
- energize and retain employees by providing new challenges in their current roles as well as preparing them for other roles

- conduct more focused planning sessions because the employees are better prepared
- create roles for experienced employees as mentors and/or informal trainers for less-experienced employees
- create low-cost customized learning opportunities through assignments
- respond to employee-initiated requests for specialized feedback

✓ The organization benefits because:
- support for individual development planning is a competitive advantage in attracting and retaining employees and maximizing employee motivation and productivity
- more specific and accurate information about employee interests and goals is available to assist with future resource planning and succession planning
- it can plan for and assign training dollars more realistically
- developmental planning creates more effective internal networks of people seeking out others for advice and information

57

Leadership Development: Training

The focus is on helping an employee become strong, not about making the
employee feel better about being weak.

—Chip Bell, *Managers as Mentors*

Leaders are the key agents in translating training and learning outcomes into
real workplace results. They are responsible for linking skills development to
business results. A leader has three key roles with regard to employee training:

1. recommending specific training courses or activities and linking them
   to the employee's role and performance measures
2. debriefing trainees on lessons learned and linking those lessons to
   specific activities and opportunities
3. conducting follow-up through action plans and feedback soon after
   the learning of a new skill has taken place

A leader also has responsibilities to the organization in supporting training's
overall effectiveness. These include:

✓ recommending new or expanded training courses to meet business
   challenges
✓ recommending training course content, including case studies, that
   reflects the day-to-day working environment

✔ providing feedback to the course providers on how effective the trainees were after the program

Here are other ways in which leaders can strengthen the link between training
activities and organizational impact:

✔ Arrange for employees who have attended a training session to present
to their teams a short overview of key lessons.

✔ Set up a resource center of training course manuals and literature for
all employees to use as reference guides.

✔ Define your core competencies. These are the skills, if practiced, that
will improve employees' ability to contribute to the mission of the
organization.

✔ Document the core competencies that will drive performance at each
level of the organization. Have employees demonstrate how any outside
course will enhance their abilities to perform these core competencies—before they are given permission to attend the program.

✔ If formal workshops are still part of your organization's culture, ensure
that employees attend only those that have a direct bearing on your
corporate mission and core competencies.

✔ Ensure that everyone attending workshops knows the learning objectives of the sessions and can identify the link between those objectives
and their own goals.

✔ Multiply the value of workshops and conferences by ensuring that all
employees present a summary of the best ideas to other employees
members who might benefit from the learning.

✔ Spend time with people who are about to take a course to ensure that
you are aware of the course objectives and that you know what value
the learner intends to transfer back into the job. Hold them accountable for applying the new skills.

✔ Follow up with learners who have attended a workshop or conference
to identify how they intend to apply their learning. Continue to follow
up with them periodically to encourage them by providing praise as
appropriate.

✓ If your organization is piloting a new program, volunteer for the first session. Be constructive. Show enthusiasm. Ensure that the facilitator provides sufficient time to plan the next steps.

✓ If you have engaged outside facilitators, provide them with feedback that will help them fine-tune their teaching in order to have maximum impact on the organization.

Mentoring

If you would thoroughly know anything, teach it to others.
—Tryon Edwards

The best leaders enjoy helping their people to learn, grow, and succeed in their careers. At times these relationships grow into mentoring arrangements. Mentoring goes beyond simply directing or instructing others. You may find yourself taking a deeper interest in the growth and career success of some of your employees and make deliberate efforts to help them develop the skills and knowledge they need to move up the corporate ladder. Through mentoring you might even groom your own replacement for when you retire or move on to another opportunity.

Mentors are advisers, teachers, sounding boards, cheerleaders, and critics all rolled into one. Through mentoring you give those who are less experienced an opportunity to improve their understanding of business practices, understand the organization's politics, discuss problems, analyze and learn from mistakes, and celebrate successes. Leaders should be expected to share their wisdom with people from other parts of the organization, known as protégés or mentees. Protégés tend to learn more quickly than they would through the normal process of trial and error. Here are strategies to use as a mentor.

✓ Consider your mentoring commitment carefully.
  • Don't agree to mentor someone if you don't have the time or the interest. It's flattering to be asked to be a mentor, but ask yourself

whether you are sincerely interested in and committed to helping those who are less experienced to benefit from your knowledge and experience.

- Be clear about how much time you are able to give to a mentoring relationship.
- If a formal mentoring relationship doesn't appeal to you or if you are unable to make the commitment because of time constraints, say so and consider whether you can recommend someone else in your network as a prospective mentor.

✓ Look for informal as well as formal mentoring opportunities.

- Consider whether your company would benefit from a formal mentoring program. Some organizations establish a system whereby senior members of employees advise and guide junior workers in order to help with succession planning and expedite professional development. In other cases, mentor-protégé relationships evolve spontaneously and are carried on as informal arrangements.
- For less formal mentoring relationships, watch for when your employees are receptive to receiving advice or coaching. These opportunities often present themselves when employees are struggling with a problem, are dealing with the consequences of a mistake or bad decision, or express a desire to grow.
- Allow mentoring relationships to evolve naturally. Unless you have already known your protégé for quite some time, it's unlikely that you will immediately feel at ease in communicating with him or her. It takes time for any relationship to develop.

✓ Establish clear goals for formal mentoring relationships. Some people seek out a mentor because they know it's a good career move, but beyond that aren't really clear about what they want.

- When someone asks you to be a mentor, ask him to articulate clearly what he wants to get out of the relationship. At the beginning of your formal relationship, ask your protégé for a written goal statement. Why has he chosen you to be a mentor? What skills, abilities, or knowledge does he want to develop? How does he want you to help with his goals? What are his expectations of you in terms of time? In the eyes of your protégé, what would constitute success?

- Create a "contract" with the protégé to include:
  - frequency of meetings
  - notice of cancellation
  - confidentiality
  - topics that would be off limits
- Each time you meet, ask for an update on your protégé's progress. Has she followed up on any assignments or actions you have recommended? What went well or didn't go well? What could be improved the next time? What has your protégé learned from recent experiences?
- At regular intervals, revisit the goals your protégé chose and determine if they are still valid or need updating.

✓ Establish a pace that seems reasonable.
- Don't try to "download" all your knowledge and experience in only a few sessions with your protégé. Remember that you didn't learn everything at once.
- Keep your mentoring discussions focused on relevant goals or challenges that your protégé is facing. Learning is often most effective when delivered just in time.

✓ Be accessible.
- Establish a schedule for contact that is both feasible for you and meets the needs of your protégé. You may choose to meet weekly, biweekly, or monthly. You have to meet with your protégé regularly to monitor his progress and to be sufficiently involved that you can give relevant advice.
- Establish parameters for when you are available for consultation by e-mail or voice mail between mentoring sessions.

✓ Don't aim to create a clone of yourself.
  • Offer your own ideas based on your experience, but don't expect that your protégé will necessarily do things exactly the way you would.
  • Encourage creative, individual thinking. Let your protégé try her own approach, even if you aren't sure that it will work.

✓ Be an encouraging confidant.
  • Encourage your protégé to aim for high standards and push her to set challenging goals. Continue raising the bar when you feel that she is ready to stretch even further.
  • Balance praise with constructive criticism. Your role as a mentor is to both support and challenge your protégé.
  • If something your protégé tries doesn't turn out as expected, help with the postmortem analysis, but remind her that mistakes are part of the learning and growth process.
  • Treat your discussions as confidential. Your protégé may confide in you much more than the average employee. You may hear information that you wouldn't normally hear. Respect the trust that your protégé has placed in you by keeping all the information shared in your discussions confidential.
  • Acknowledge and celebrate your protégé's achievements. Less experienced workers may not recognize the significance of what they have achieved.

✓ Don't give all the answers.
  • When your protégé asks for your help with a problem, ask him to suggest several possible approaches. Encourage discussion and exploration of these various courses of action, raising any significant concerns or points your protégé might have missed.
  • Influence your protégé to take a specific direction only if you feel he might be about to choose a disastrous course of action. Otherwise encourage your protégé to make the choices and decisions that he feels are best.

✓ Know when it's time to let go.

- Your protégé may be reluctant to tell you that he has outgrown you or may simply be unaware that it is time to move on. You may need to suggest that your official work together as mentor and protégé is coming to an end. Your mentoring relationship may end because you or your protégé moves to another department or company. Or it may just become clear that your protégé has learned everything he can learn from you. Some mentors and protégés become lifelong friends. Other mentoring relationships simply devolve in the same way that they evolved.

- Help your protégé to plan for the future before ending your formal mentoring relationship. How does she plan to continue growing and progressing? Are there other people in your network who might be able to help your protégé with the next phase of her career?

Motivating Others

He who loses money, loses much; he who loses a friend,
loses much more; he who loses faith, loses all.

—Eleanor Roosevelt

As a leader, your treatment of others will have a major impact on their enthusiasm and commitments. Here are some things you can do to bring out the best in people.

✓ Have high expectations. The more you expect from people, the greater the effort they will make. Your trust in people will ensure that you give them leeway to do things their way.

✓ Listen. Keep your ear to the ground. Identify issues that might cause poor morale and take swift action to deal decisively with problems. Set aside time to hold focus groups to allow people to identify concerns that you can address on their behalf.

✓ Recognize superior effort and achievement. Show your appreciation soon, by being specific about the achievement and in a personal way. You can show your pleasure in dozens of ways, including:
- private verbal appreciation
- public recognition
- a handwritten note
- an e-mail with a copy to someone really important
- a note in the person's file

✓ Pay people well. If possible, overpay people—it will provide valuable return on the investment. People who feel underpaid never give 100 percent. In fact, they give as little as possible. Keeping salaries low seldom ends up in lower costs.

✓ Pay attention to your language and the way you treat people. You are the role model, and others will evaluate your behavior.

  • Refer to employees as "our people," or associates, not "full-time equivalents (FTEs)" or other demeaning ways of referring to people.

  • Have a human resources department, not a personnel department. Better still, rename it something exciting, such as the "department of people potential."

  • Ensure that the head of human resources is an executive position, reporting directly to the president, not the chief financial officer.

✓ Treat your people with respect.

  • Ask them—don't question them.

  • Measure their performance instead of monitoring them.

  • Sell them ideas. Don't just tell them to implement your ideas, especially if they are likely to be unpopular.

  • View them as contributors, not costs.

  • Regard them as needed, not tolerated.

✓ Award spontaneous bonuses for exceptional achievement. Don't publicize the process, in case you create expectations. Pay bonuses in various amounts at different times so that they are a surprise and seen as genuine appreciation for a job well done.

✓ Set goals with employees; they need to know what you expect of them. Document those goals and monitor progress toward them.

✓ Remember your employees' partners. Often your people will be called on to put in extra effort that may require them to work longer hours or over a weekend. Send the significant other some acknowledgement in return for their support, such as a card, flowers, or a voucher for a meal for two. If you're on the road and have invited employees to dinner, offer to host their partners too.

✓ Have fun. Look for opportunities where people can get together and laugh. Business is serious, but people will be more motivated if they have reason to smile.

Rewards and Recognition

Men are rich only as they give. He who gives great service gets great rewards.
                                                                —Elbert Hubbard

The rewards dished out by senior executives have a significant impact on the performance culture of an organization, since they send clear messages about behaviors that are valued.

A key leadership skill is to create heroes among the people who excel. The benefits are motivational and significant, although the cost of doing so is often next to nothing. Here is a list of principles that will enhance the effectiveness of rewards and recognition.

- ✓ Make a distinction between rewards and recognition. "Rewards" are the benefits given to employees for specific achievements—their own, their team's, or the organization's. "Recognition" consists of rewards given by individual supervisors to their people for superior perform-ance. The recognition is usually spontaneous and is typically informal.
- ✓ Senior managers design reward systems. To be effective they need to be linked to measurable results, organizational values, or core compe-tencies. Key performance indicators typically relate to benefits for one or more of the stakeholders—customers, shareholders, and employees.
- ✓ Designing a reward system is tricky, to say the least, especially when money is concerned.
  - Consider rewarding teams as much as you do individuals. This will encourage collaborative behavior.
  - Do recognize your individual stars, but do so less publicly.

✓ Involve your employees in the design of a reward system. It's going to be impossible to please everyone, but widespread involvement will ensure that your system is:

- acceptable to most
- relevant (rewards should include items, both cash and noncash, that will be regarded as useful)
- fair (there is nothing worse than a system that is seen to be inequitable)

✓ Increase the potency of your employee recognition by:

- demonstrating the types of recognition you value yourself
- doing so spontaneously
- including flexibility for managers by giving them a budget and discretion for recognition

✓ In providing recognition to employees, you should:

- avoid giving rewards for things that are already being done effectively
- reward only superior performance
- focus more on actions that are not part of the normal routine and that might be considered "over and above"
- provide timely feedback

✓ Make sure that people know specifically why they are being rewarded.

✓ Avoid patronizing when giving verbal recognition. People will know that you are not being genuine when you:

- exaggerate the extent of their achievements
- use a tone of voice and gestures that are inconsistent with your verbal message
- stretch the truth by using overblown language such as "always," "never," or "phenomenal" to describe performance that is only just above average

Retaining High Performers

A wise man will make more opportunities than he finds.
—Sir Francis Bacon

Senior leaders all have one task in common—responsibility for supporting employee development while growing organizational capacity. Too often, however, confronting poor performers takes attention and energy away from the more important priority: to encouraging good performers to excel. The result can shortchange the loyal and committed people responsible for past and future successes.

✓ High performers are a greater liability to your organization if they don't get meaningful attention and support, because it's their attitude and energy that set the standards for others.

✓ It's pretty easy to "turn off" your high performers. Here are some deadly phrases that leaders inadvertently use without appreciating the consequences:

  • "Let's get your evaluation over with . . . thank goodness I don't have any issues with you."
  • "I know you won't like this assignment but I've got no time to train someone else."
  • "I can't possibly let you go on training . . . no one can do your job while you're gone."

- "I know that what I've given you is a stretch, but you'll figure it out."
- "If you think you have a crummy job, then spend one day in my shoes. You'll see that being the boss is even worse."

✓ What to do if you've been even a little guilty of that behavior? Here are some quick fixes that can make a long-term difference:

- *Love in the Workplace.* Spend some time finding out what people love to do, and create assignments that bring a balance of risk and excitement to their roles. You know what they can do, but not what they love. Put passion back into performance!

- *Promote from Within.* Use your networks and influence to create an opportunity for a high performer to serve in a high-profile or executive role in an industry or professional association. Reward performance with enhanced networks, influence, and leadership challenges.

- *Be a Matchmaker.* Create an opportunity for a high performer to have an information meeting with someone who is a business role model, or create a customized mentoring partnership with a senior manager. (You'll learn a lot about someone's ambitions and values when you learn about her role models.)

- *Publish or Perish.* Reproduce a speech or project that your high performer has undertaken. Make it look professional and attractive and give the performer lots of extra copies for his portfolio. And don't forget, your organization's name gets some circulation too.

- *Train to Gain.* Go beyond the standard course offerings. Send the high performer off to a unique course that develops an area of interest that she is passionate about even though it may only be indirectly related to her job. These courses are more energizing and personal than expensive executive-development courses, and are far more likely to keep someone attached to the organization.

- *Life Before the Exit Interview.* Exit interviews happen too late! Why not approach some high performers and acknowledge that you're pleased they've stayed? Find out what you and your organization do well, and how you can do those things more often and even better. It's an enormous compliment to be approached for honest discussion and acknowledgment of one's worth.

In a nutshell, good performers need feedback, encouragement, and acknowledgment. These strategies are simple and inexpensive, especially when you compare them to the cost of replacing good talent. An effective leader turns good performance into great outcomes. And that's the real satisfaction of leadership today.

PART 5

Performance Leadership

Leadership is the art of getting someone else to do something you want done
because he wants to do it.

—Dwight D. Eisenhower

Most organizations have a mission. Ideally that mission has been documented
and articulated by the organization's leaders. Having done so, they must create
an atmosphere and systems that enable people, equipment, and materials to come
together to make products and services that are best in class. Chapters 62 through
69 provide the ingredients for successfully driving performance improvement.

Accountability and Responsibility: Getting the Monkey off Your Back

Purposeful organizations are exciting, inspiring places to work. Purpose inspires even the most mundane task with meaning.

—Lorin Woolfe, *The Bible on Leadership*

Too often we describe the ideal leader as tough, decisive, and assertive. He's in charge—certainly a good model for getting things done in a hurry. Indeed, in urgent situations this is the appropriate approach. But a different style would work better in situations where there's time to deal with complex situations, when creativity and commitment are important!

The collaborative approach has other, long-lasting benefits—it spreads responsibility to those who need to take ownership. Performance is unlikely to be at an acceptable level without that sense of ownership. To increase feelings of ownership, leaders need to do the following:

✓ Clearly define which decisions are to be taken by one person or a few, and which require more general acceptance.
✓ Identify and document (in job descriptions) the aspects of performance that the individual employee is accountable for. Wherever possible, measurable indicators should be established to track whether that person is performing according to expectations. (See Chapter 63, "Accountability: Measuring Outcomes.")

✓ Define responsibilities at the end of every meeting. As decisions are being made, a secretary/recorder should note exactly what commitments have been made, who undertook to do what, and when it is to be done. "ASAP" or "soon" is not a commitment!

✓ Provide feedback when commitments are met—and especially when they are not. People need to know which obligations are taken seriously. As a leader, your attitude toward meeting obligations will send a clear message about what is important. If you are seen to accept ongoing nonfulfillment of obligations, you will breed a culture of laissez-faire performers. Letting people know about your disappointment when deadlines are missed is important too. Consider involving your team in deciding how to deal with "breaches of contract." Often a small fine, such as a dollar for coming late to a meeting, is sufficient punishment for infractions. This highlights the transgression instead of accepting it as "normal" or acceptable.

Accountability:
Measuring Outcomes

Not everything that counts can be counted.
Not everything that is counted counts.

—-Albert Einstein

Accountability and measurement are inseparable concepts. You can't hold people accountable until you measure their effectiveness. The question then becomes how to get employees to take ownership of measures and goals. Should we involve the people who are responsible? Yes, involving those who participate in the delivery of the service or product clearly builds ownership and motivation to do better. Traditional measurement systems have long failed to work because they are based on the flawed philosophy that only managers can know the measures of success and are capable of setting goals and ensuring that the targets are achieved.

It is no secret that what you measure will improve—sometimes. There are times when people see measurement as a way of exercising control over them. In such cases the system will breed resentment and possibly dishonest behavior, with employees manipulating the statistics in order to report good numbers instead of the truth.

Here is how to use measurement to motivate:

✓ Measure all the things that are important to you.
✓ What is important is that the needs of all the stakeholders be met.

Choose indicators that measure success in satisfying the customers, shareholders, management, and the employees.

✓ In choosing indicators, find a balance among those that measure the past (financial), the present (service), and the future (learning and innovation).

✓ Involve stakeholders in choosing the appropriate indicators. This will ensure greater buy-in and ownership of the process.

✓ Establish the effectiveness of your organization's performance with regard to each indicator. Consider benchmarking your performance against others in the industry. Or, better still, benchmark your organization against those from other industries that have similar processes. This may help you identify new possibilities that are perhaps not part of the standard way of doing things in your industry. In order to get maximum buy-in to the new possibilities, ensure that your employees are part of the information-gathering team.

✓ Now that you know the possibilities, set challenging goals. Goals also need to be specific, measurable, agreed upon, realistic (yet challenging), and time-based (SMART).

✓ Display the measures so that everyone can see them.

✓ Form miniteams for each key success factor. Have each team take responsibility for collecting the data each month and looking for new, innovative ways of improving the scores.

✓ Meet regularly to review performance. Compare actual performance against goals.

✓ Celebrate significant gains (see Chapter 60, "Rewards and Recognition") and involve process owners in finding solutions for either declines in performance or performance that needs to improve.

Creativity, Innovation, and Continuous Improvement

> The definition of insanity is doing things over and
> over again and expecting different results.
>
> —Benjamin Franklin

Creativity, innovation, and continuous improvement are all intertwined concepts that aim at moving an organization forward on the road to perfection. Although the ultimate destination is elusive, the process of getting there nevertheless continues. It is particularly important that leaders focus on incremental improvements and create the climate and processes for this to occur.

Innovation and creativity are similar but different. Innovation leads to improving an existing product or service, adding to it, making it perform better, more quickly, and/or at less cost. Creativity, on the other hand, causes something unique to come into being—an original idea.

✓ As a leader you have a special responsibility to provide the climate for new ideas to percolate up, be examined, and be implemented, if justified. Consider the following issues as clues to whether you have done so.
  - Do you challenge (stretch) people when setting goals rather simply being satisfied with past achievements?
  - Do people have a measurable degree of freedom to pursue new ideas?

- Are employees given time to try new ideas during work hours?
- Would you describe your environment as trusting and open, allowing people with different perspectives equal opportunities to access resources and influence decision makers?
- How do you deal with conflict? Do you prefer to sweep it under the carpet? Do employees personalize the issues and beat up on people whose ideas are different from their own? Or do you respect all ideas, listen to them, and consider their merits, trying to find them from a variety of sources? And do you welcome conflict, knowing that it is permissible—and important—to have a variety of opinions, because they produce a better outcome?

✓ Take active steps to promote new initiatives.
- Involve employees at every level. They all bring a variety of ideas to work, some of which could have big payoffs. Leave idea boards and flip charts around the workplace to encourage people to record new ideas as they come to them. Then examine these ideas at ongoing meetings.
- Set aside time at each meeting specifically for new ideas. Let the more outlandish ideas percolate before dismissing them, since someone else may be able to add to the idea, turning it into a winning proposition.
- Seek out ideas from outside the organization. The NIH (not invented here) syndrome has little merit. Copy ideas from different industries when the product or service may provide added value to your clients.
- Bring in experts when needed, especially from the outside. These people are likely to have a different perspective and will tend to see more opportunities than obstacles. And many obstacles are more about perception than reality.
- Establish and communicate criteria for new ideas. Cost ceilings, payback periods, and discretionary spending for innovation should be known to all. In this way a host of new ideas can be fairly quickly whittled down to the best prospects.

- Set targets for new products and services. Establish goals for each area of your organization to make people aware that innovation is important. Challenge and reward individuals and teams that bring new ideas to fruition.
- Measure your efforts and successes. In your matrix of measures include indicators that track the organization's abilities in this area. Possible indicators include:
  - number of new ideas generated per period
  - percentage of new ideas implemented
  - average evaluation time for new ideas
  - number of new ideas per employee per period
  - revenue growth from new services and products
  - number of patent submissions per period
  - climate for innovation, as measured by a survey comprising questions about whether the atmosphere encourages or discourages innovation

Post these measures so that people are aware of them and can observe trends indicating improvement or deterioration.
- Institutionalize the creation of new ideas. Without creating a bureaucracy or sole ownership for innovation, ensure that dedicated resource people are working on new projects that will keep you one (or more) steps ahead of the competition.
- Set up programs to encourage new ideas. Especially if your organization is spread around the world, provide opportunities—such as knowledge-sharing fairs—for people to get together and share best practices.
- Celebrate failures. Acknowledge the effort and initiative even if an idea does not pan out the way everyone would have liked.

High-Performance Leadership

The ultimate destination for all leaders is sustainable value creation.
—Noel M. Tichy, *The Cycle of Leadership*

Day by day, leaders focus on energizing all their resources in pursuing their dreams—the visions—by executing their missions. Their strategies can ensure that the organization continues to add value to all stakeholders—clients, management, and employees. This necessitates creating a high-performance culture. Here are some strategies that will make the difference:

✓ Ensure that all managers are able to coach their people daily. This means that they:
  - set goals with individuals and with teams
  - measure key performance indicators
  - follow up regularly to monitor progress
  - provide ongoing feedback to employees when performance exceeds or fails to meet expectations
  - give regular formal feedback on employee performance

✓ Identify the different core competencies for each level of management. Top management needs to be more strategic, middle management more organizational, and first-level management more technical in nature. Make sure the performance-management system incorporates these competencies so that managers are:

- rewarded for demonstrating those abilities
- given training or other help to acquire them

✓ Ensure that any formal training—in technical or managerial skills—is aligned with the core competencies.

✓ After training sessions, follow up with employees to find out what they learned and how they intend to apply their new skills back on the job. Monitor progress and recognize improvements.

✓ Ensure that employees are given an opportunity to participate in decisions, especially those who promote continuous improvement. Ensure that all your managers are trained to hold meetings where they:
- review operating data with employees
- celebrate improvements
- solicit new ideas that will improve operations
- plan implementation of new ideas

✓ Encourage the transfer of innovative new practices among departments. Hold regular meetings to review performance, celebrating achievements and sharing best practices.

✓ Ensure that every employee has specific, measurable, agreed-upon, realistic (yet challenging), and time-based (SMART) goals. Each one should have goals that are reviewed with his supervisor at least at monthly intervals.

✓ Display key measures of the company's success in important locations, such as the entrances to the building and the cafeteria, so that people are aware of how the organization is doing.

✓ Employees who have demonstrated above-average performance improvements and have taken risks to change the way business is conducted should be treated like folk heroes.

✓ Generate enthusiasm by projecting excitement when appropriate. Leaders smile, raise their voices, and have good eye contact when presenting important ideas, and smile, lean forward, and listen carefully to others who display enthusiasm.

High-Performance Organizations

I am careful not to confuse excellence with perfection. Excellence,
I can reach for; perfection is God's business.

—Michael J. Fox

Leaders continuously challenge the status quo, seldom satisfied with what they have achieved. They strive for excellence in everything they do. And they expect the same from others. They also realize that there is no secret to success. Instead they understand that the key building blocks for top performance include:

✓ *Focusing on the Customer*. Success comes not from being all things to all people but from picking areas where unique value can be created for customers. Customers are valued above all else.

✓ *Creating the Right Organizational Structure*. Leaders build their organizations not around themselves but around the customer. In order to create consistently reliable, fast service, they structure people into teams that control and "own" each key product or service to ensure that processes flows quickly and flawlessly.

✓ *Making Management Lean*. The fewer the layers, the better, simply because the alternative will encourage more bureaucracy, meetings, policies, poor coordination, and withdrawal of power from the people who need it—those who serve the customer.

✓ *Aligning Measurement and Reward Systems with the Mission*. Most organizations have a mission, but few actually measure whether they are doing what they profess to want to do. Fewer still use measurement to motivate employees. By involving employees in the following, measurement will become a motivational force, not a tool for control and punishment:

- identifying the critical indicators
- allowing them to collect data
- displaying results for all to see
- meeting regularly to review results
- celebrating improvements
- involving employees in finding new ways to improve performance

Layoffs

All paid jobs absorb and degrade the mind.

—Aristotle

There is little evidence to support the notion that wholesale cuts to the number of people in an organization do more than create favorable optics for the shareholders in the short term. It certainly does little to benefit the other key stakeholders in the medium and long term. Why? It's usually the people with the longest years of experience—the most costly—who are let go first. Since downsizing typically happens suddenly, and secretively, organizations are rarely prepared to deal with the skills vacuum that results. Customer service is disrupted, causing more lost business, which in turn will result in more layoffs. The process keeps repeating itself until a leader emerges who is bent on building the business and realizes the value of people in the strategy.

But there are times when reduction of jobs may be necessary, either because the nature of the business has changed, the market has contracted, some aspects of the business have been outsourced, or economic conditions have deteriorated. In such circumstances it is critical that the layoffs be made compassionately. The fellow employees who remain will be those whose loyalty and commitment during the transition to a leaner operating structure will be crucial.

Here are some basic principles that should guide the process:

✓ Anticipate trends. Focus on the future so that new challenges are anticipated. Prepare people for those changes so that they are trained for the new roles that might emerge and can walk away from jobs that have become redundant.

✓ Keep communications open and honest. Give people as much information as possible that has an impact on job security. But don't use possible job losses as a way of threatening people into changing or becoming more productive.

✓ If layoffs are necessary, encourage people to stay with the organization until the process is wound up in an orderly manner.

✓ Reward people for staying until the end, especially as they may have sacrificed opportunities to find alternative employment.

✓ If possible, rather than laying them off, transfer people to other divisions of your organization.

✓ Make a concerted effort to place as many of your people as possible in jobs within the community. If necessary, approach other organizations directly and offer them the opportunity to bring some of your best talent on board.

✓ Assist those who cannot be placed by providing them with resources to help them find new careers.

✓ Offer medical benefits for as long as possible.

✓ Keep employees informed if closing dates change.

✓ Treat people as generously as possible. When they leave they should feel that they have been treated fairly and respectfully.

✓ Retain valuable knowledge. Before deciding to retrench people because of their costs to the organization, review the knowledge that you may be losing and the cost of replacing it. Consider also the potential damage if the unique knowledge that they carry in their heads is downloaded into the knowledge base of a competitor.

✓ In the event that individuals must be terminated, ensure that it is done as professionally as possible, by people schooled in the process. This will reduce the potential costs—already considerable—of a court judgment that punishes you more severely than expected. Use these approaches to reduce animosity:

- Ensure that employees are not marched off the premises in front of fellow workers—an unnecessarily humiliating process.
- Avoid firing people late on a Friday, as this will deprive them of opportunities to tap into support resources that will help cushion the blow.
- Be aware of important events or personal troubles in employees' lives, and avoid firing during these times if at all possible.

Learning Organizations

You must learn from the mistakes of others.
You can't possibly live long enough to make them all yourself.
—Sam Levenson (1911–1980)

Most organizations have human resources departments. The concept of human resources suggests that employees are assets that can be nurtured, grown, and developed. In fact, reality is most often the opposite. When budgets are cut, training is usually the first to go—even though most executives realize that knowledge is a key competitive weapon.

Creating a learning organization—one in which people accumulate knowledge that makes them and the organization more effective—is not a question of sending people to more workshops. On the contrary, formal learning is only a small part of the development equation. Here is a list of alternative strategies to develop knowledge.

✓ Encourage continuous learning. Ensure that the primary focus of annual performance reviews is the future, not the past. Have your managers create for each individual learning plans that will promote continuous learning from a variety of sources.

✓ Create self-directed learning teams. Encourage employees who enjoy training to form volunteer learning groups that meet regularly (for example, monthly) to learn from each other. These meetings should:

- be conducted informally, allowing lots of time for discussion and transfer of opinions and best practices
- be facilitated on a rotating basis by one person at a time
- deal with topics chosen by the group
- typically not be more than two hours in length
- involve groups of six to ten members—all volunteers
- include members from different work areas, promoting cross-pollination of ideas and breaking down barriers among work areas
- cover bite-sized topics, including managerial, business, and even technical subjects
- give members time between meetings to apply their learning

✓ Constantly survey stakeholders—both customers and employees—to identify new opportunities to serve them better. Prioritize the opportunities. Establish task forces to recommend solutions. Have line employees take responsibility for implementing these ideas.

✓ Use measurement to promote learning. Measure performance in each area of the organization and display charts of key performance indicators for all to see. Meet regularly with employees to review performance. If it has improved, establish what new things have brought about the improvement. Document them. Make them a part of ongoing standards. If performance has declined, find out why and ask what can be done to avoid that happening again. Get agreement to those ideas and create plans for improvement. By getting employees involved in proposing innovations you are promoting learning about the nature of your systems.

✓ Celebrate innovative actions, even those that prove to be mistakes. That's right! Encourage people to try new ideas. But turn failures into positive experiences by analyzing what went wrong and how the mistake can be avoided next time. Needless to say, actions with the potential for major mistakes—such as those involving the health and safety of employees—should always be avoided.

✓ Meet regularly with fellow managers, inside and outside your organization, to establish best practices. Keep an open mind to new ideas, even when at first glance they don't seem to fit your circumstances. Share some of these new ideas with your people and invite their feedback. Allow ideas to percolate until they are dismissed, used in part, or fully adapted.

✓ Encourage your managers to learn from each other and to maximize the value of learning from whatever sources they use. Reward managers who share ideas openly.

✓ Conduct ongoing benchmarking of key processes. But get the most value at the least cost by:

- Allowing your employees to define what they could best learn from other organizations.
- Identifying organizations that have similar processes but are in another industry (you're bound to find fresh ideas).
- Allowing your employees, not a consultant, to do the data collection. This will increase enthusiasm for and commitment to implement the new ideas.

✓ Find a mentor and allow others to avail themselves of this learning format too. Seek someone inside or outside your organization whose life and business skills complement yours. Give yourself the opportunity to share ideas with someone who will just listen (a sounding board) or who could offer you advice in areas of personal weakness (an advisor).

Measurement:
The Balanced Scorecard

There are three kinds of lies: lies, damned lies, and statistics.
—Benjamin Disraeli, British politician (1804–1881)

In recent years the concept of the "Balanced Scorecard" has gained ground as a powerful tool to improve organizational performance. Created by David Norton and Robert Kaplan, the system has become a favorite of CEOs for these reasons:

✓ The system requires that a vision and a mission be created at the outset. The scorecard is then created to track your ability to do what you have professed to be important. Measurement systems created without a linkage to the mission are often one-sided, favoring one stakeholder or another.

✓ The system uses the input of the people who must take ownership for improvements in performance.

✓ A balanced scorecard measures a variety of issues, some of which focus on the past (financial success) and others that focus on the future (learning and innovation).

✓ Balance is created by measuring whether all the stakeholders have been satisfied—the shareholders, the employees, and the customers.

✓ The system requires you to think about the future and to set challenging goals. After creating key performance indicators (KPIs), employees are able to meet regularly and track whether they are making progress.

The Balanced Scorecard can have a number of formats. A simple and effective system is known as the Performance Index.

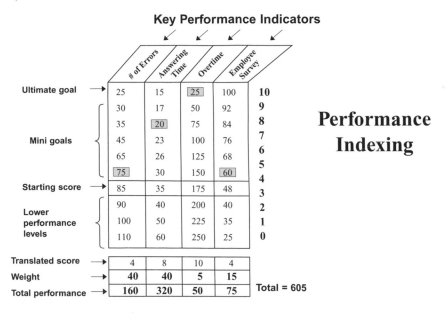

Key Performance Indicators

	# of Errors	Answering Time	Overtime	Employee Survey	
Ultimate goal →	25	15	25	100	**10**
	30	17	50	92	**9**
	35	20	75	84	**8**
Mini goals	45	23	100	76	**7**
	65	26	125	68	**6**
	75	30	150	60	**5**
Starting score →	85	35	175	48	**4**
Lower performance levels	90	40	200	40	**2**
	100	50	225	35	**1**
	110	60	250	25	**0**
Translated score →	4	8	10	4	
Weight →	40	40	5	15	
Total performance →	160	320	50	75	**Total = 605**

Performance Indexing

A group sets up a Performance Index by following a step-by-step process:

1. Define the mission of the organization. This statement describes *what* the organization is trying to do, *how* it does it, *who* it serves, *why* it does so, and *where* it operates.
2. Identify the KPIs and write them on the chart (see the sample Performance Index above). KPIs relate directly to the mission and define how the stakeholders will judge their level of satisfaction. Ideal performance indicators will:
   ✓ be readily available
   ✓ be easy to collect
   ✓ be accurate
   ✓ measure things the stakeholders have control over

   In some cases accurate data will not be available, so data-collection systems will have to be established.

3. Establish current performance levels. Systems for collecting accurate data need to be in place if they are not already established.

    ✓ Set goals with the involvement of staff to encourage them to "own" them. These goals should change the team and be as specific as possible.

    ✓ Goals are set at the score level ten, the ultimate success level.

4. Determine minigoals and then insert them between the start and the goal level (levels three and ten). This can be done arithmetically to create equal steps between the current level of performance and the twelve-month goal.

5. Determine lower performance levels. Decide how much poorer performance could be if it actually declined. Although it is hoped that this will not occur, it is entirely possible that performance will not always improve, especially in cyclical or seasonal operations. These lower scores are written in at levels zero to two.

6. Establish the relative importance of the various items. Depending on how important it is seen to be, each indicator will be given a percentage and their weights will add up to 100 percent. In many organizations the customer indicators are given a significant weight. In others the weights are distributed equally among all the stakeholders.

7. Plan for improvement. The challenge begins when the stakeholders identify the roadblocks that stand in front of their goals. They systematically plan to remove them, one at a time. They should also look outside of their operations for ideas that will help them improve dramatically. (See Chapter 29, "Benchmarking").

8. Meet regularly to review progress. Stakeholders should get together monthly to evaluate their progress. They should celebrate their accomplishments and identify root causes and solutions for problems that they encounter along the way. The group should also document new actions that have contributed to improved performance, as well as actions that have caused deterioration in performance. In this way they become a *learning team* that is knowledgeable about the factors that contribute to their successes.

Index